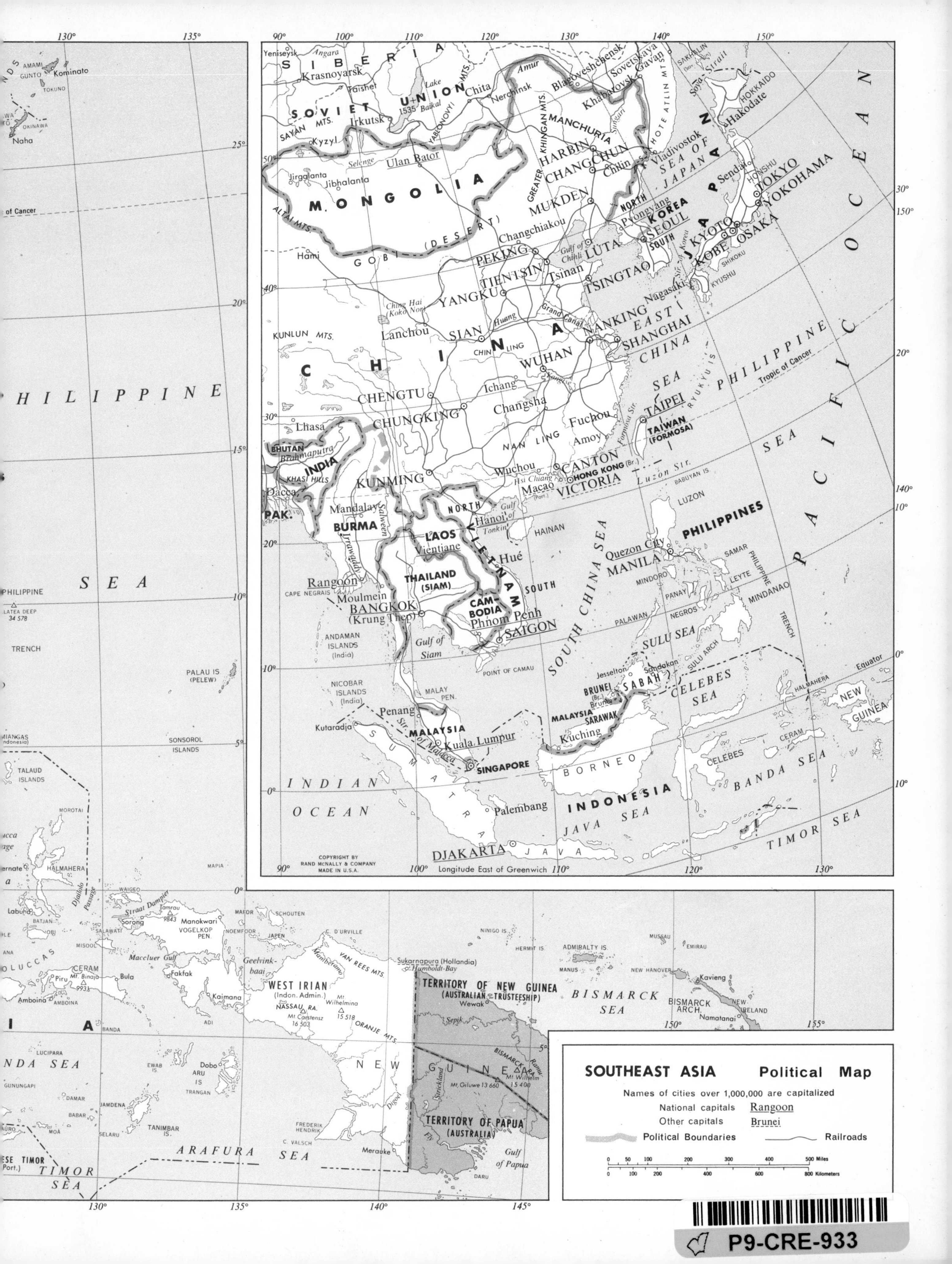
SOUTHEAST ASIA Political Map
Names of cities over 1,000,000 are capitalized
National capitals Rangoon
Other capitals Brunei
Political Boundaries
Railroads
0 50 100 200 300 400 500 Miles
0 100 200 400 600 800 Kilometers
Longitude East of Greenwich
COPYRIGHT BY RAND McNALLY & COMPANY MADE IN U.S.A.
SOVIET UNION
SIBERIA
Krasnoyarsk
Irkutsk
Chita
Nerchinsk
Blagoveshchensk
Khabarovsk
Sovetskaya Gavan
Vladivostok
MONGOLIA
Ulan Bator
GOBI (DESERT)
MANCHURIA
HARBIN
CHANGCHUN
MUKDEN
NORTH KOREA
Pyongyang
SOUTH KOREA
SEOUL
SEA OF JAPAN
JAPAN
TOKYO
YOKOHAMA
KYOTO
OSAKA
KOBE
Sendai
Hakodate
HOKKAIDO
HONSHU
SHIKOKU
KYUSHU
Nagasaki
CHINA
PEKING
TIENTSIN
Changchiakou
LUTA
TSINGTAO
Tsinan
YANGKU
Lanchou
SIAN
NANKING
SHANGHAI
WUHAN
CHENGTU
CHUNGKING
Ichang
Changsha
Fuchou
Amoy
Wuchou
CANTON
KUNMING
Lhasa
Hami
KUNLUN MTS.
CHIN LING
NAN LING
EAST CHINA SEA
TAIPEI
TAIWAN (FORMOSA)
HONG KONG (Br.)
VICTORIA
Macao (Port.)
BHUTAN
INDIA
KHASI HILLS
Dacca
PAK.
BURMA
Mandalay
Rangoon
Moulmein
LAOS
Vientiane
NORTH VIETNAM
Hanoi
Hué
SOUTH VIETNAM
THAILAND (SIAM)
BANGKOK (Krung Thep)
CAMBODIA
Phnom Penh
SAIGON
HAINAN
Gulf of Tonkin
Gulf of Siam
ANDAMAN ISLANDS (India)
NICOBAR ISLANDS (India)
MALAY PEN.
Penang
MALAYSIA
Kuala Lumpur
SINGAPORE
SUMATRA
Kutaradja
Palembang
DJAKARTA
JAVA
JAVA SEA
INDONESIA
BORNEO
Kuching
SARAWAK
BRUNEI
SABAH
Jesselton
Sandakan
SOUTH CHINA SEA
PHILIPPINES
MANILA
Quezon City
LUZON
MINDORO
PANAY
NEGROS
PALAWAN
LEYTE
SAMAR
MINDANAO
SULU SEA
CELEBES SEA
CELEBES
CERAM
HALMAHERA
BANDA SEA
TIMOR SEA
INDIAN OCEAN
PHILIPPINE SEA
PACIFIC OCEAN
Tropic of Cancer
Equator
WEST IRIAN (Indon. Admin.)
Sukarnapura (Hollandia)
Manokwari
Sorong
Fakfak
Kaimana
Merauke
TERRITORY OF NEW GUINEA (AUSTRALIAN TRUSTEESHIP)
Wewak
TERRITORY OF PAPUA (AUSTRALIA)
Gulf of Papua
NEW GUINEA
BISMARCK SEA
BISMARCK ARCH.
ADMIRALTY IS.
NEW IRELAND
Kavieng
Namatanai
ARAFURA SEA
TIMOR SEA
PALAU IS (PELEW)
SONSOROL ISLANDS
TALAUD ISLANDS
MOROTAI
Amboina
Naha
OKINAWA
PHILIPPINE SEA
PHILIPPINE TRENCH

LIFE WORLD LIBRARY

SOUTHEAST ASIA

LIFE WORLD LIBRARY

LIFE NATURE LIBRARY

TIME READING PROGRAM

THE LIFE HISTORY OF THE UNITED STATES

LIFE SCIENCE LIBRARY

INTERNATIONAL BOOK SOCIETY

GREAT AGES OF MAN

TIME-LIFE LIBRARY OF ART

TIME-LIFE LIBRARY OF AMERICA

LIFE WORLD LIBRARY

SOUTHEAST ASIA

by Stanley Karnow

and the Editors of

TIME-LIFE BOOKS

TIME-LIFE BOOKS NEW YORK

COVER: A bulbous
11th Century monster looms above
a present-day guide standing
in a decorated cave entrance
on the island of Bali.

ABOUT THE WRITER

Stanley Karnow, who wrote the interpretive text for this volume of the LIFE World Library, is the Far East correspondent for the Washington *Post*. He has reported from Asia since 1959, when he became chief of TIME-LIFE's China and Southeast Asia bureau in Hong Kong. He has also been a correspondent in Europe, Africa and the Middle East. A 1947 graduate of Harvard, Mr. Karnow later studied at the Sorbonne in Paris. He returned to Harvard as a Nieman Fellow in 1957 to study the problems of underdeveloped countries. He contributes articles on foreign affairs to *Encounter, New Republic, Saturday Evening Post* and other magazines.

Published simultaneously in Canada.
Library of Congress catalogue card number 62-20816.
School and library distribution by Silver Burdett Company, Morristown, New Jersey.

Contents

TIME-LIFE BOOKS

EDITOR
Maitland A. Edey
EXECUTIVE EDITOR
Jerry Korn
TEXT DIRECTOR Martin Mann
ART DIRECTOR Sheldon Cotler
CHIEF OF RESEARCH
Beatrice T. Dobie
PICTURE EDITOR
Robert G. Mason
Assistant Text Directors:
Harold C. Field, Ogden Tanner
Assistant Art Director: Arnold C. Holeywell
Assistant Chief of Research: Martha T. Goolrick

•

PUBLISHER
Rhett Austell
Associate Publisher: Walter C. Rohrer
Assistant Publisher: Carter Smith
General Manager: Joseph C. Hazen Jr.
Business Manager: John D. McSweeney
Production Manager: Louis Bronzo

•

Sales Director: Joan D. Manley
Promotion Director: Beatrice K. Tolleris
Managing Director, International: John A. Millington

LIFE WORLD LIBRARY

EDITOR: Oliver E. Allen
Editorial Staff for *Southeast Asia:*
Assistant Editor: Jay Brennan
Designer: Ben Schultz
Chief Researcher: Grace Brynolson
Researchers: Nancy Jones, Barbara Ballantine, June Omura Goldberg, Linda Wolfe, Helen R. Turvey, Ava Weekes, Mollie Cooper, Paula von Haimberger Arno, Mary Elizabeth Davidson

EDITORIAL PRODUCTION
Color Director: Robert L. Young
Copy Staff: Rosalind Stubenberg, Carol Henderson, David L. Harrison, Florence Keith
Picture Department: Dolores A. Littles, Sue Bond
Traffic: Arthur A. Goldberger
Art Assistants: John M. Woods, Eve-Ann Jones

The text for this book was written by Stanley Karnow, the picture essays by David S. Thomson. The following individuals and departments of Time Inc. gave valuable aid in the preparation of this book: LIFE staff photographers, John Dominis, Eliot Elisofon and Howard Sochurek; Editorial Production, Robert W. Boyd Jr.; Editorial Reference, Peter Draz; Picture Collection, Doris O'Neil; Photographic Laboratory, George Karas; TIME-LIFE News Service, Richard M. Clurman; Correspondents, Frank McCulloch, Loren Fessler and Helen Huang (Hong Kong), Erik Amfitheatrof (Tokyo), Peter Simms (Singapore). Assistant Reprints Editor: Paula Arno.

Introduction

The impressive kingdoms established many centuries ago by the peoples of Southeast Asia, their creative genius as reflected in their sculptures, brilliant paintings and magnificent architecture, their fascinating customs, their colorful costumes, their diverse languages—all are vividly described by the author in this handsome and instructive volume. The ancient flow of religious and cultural influences into this region of Asia from India and, to a lesser extent, from China is a fascinating historical story. During the ensuing centuries these influences have, of course, become blended with the traditions and customs of the various racial and ethnic groups of Southeast Asia. But the religious influences—Hinduism, Buddhism and Christianity, and the teachings of the prophet Mohammed and of the sage Confucius—have had a profound effect. They have become deeply woven into every aspect of the lives of the people and have given them their moral codes and standards, formulated their systems of rule and government and inspired great artistic creations.

Westerners came into Southeast Asia, conquered, and built great colonial empires. Much of colonialism was marked by exploitation; a modicum of benefits began to reach peoples of these lands only toward the end of the 19th and the beginning of the 20th Century.

Inevitably, resentment against such misrule sparked the formation of secret political groups dedicated to the cause of independence and freedom. The Japanese invasion of Southeast Asia during World War II shattered the image of the "invincible white man" and set loose the pent-up force of nationalism.

Skillfully manipulating and utilizing this nationalistic fervor, the Communists, particularly the Chinese, have sought to gain control of these newly formed governments who are faced with problems of internal politics, lack of capital, lack of trained personnel and lack of industry. In North Vietnam they have temporarily succeeded. In other countries they continue their efforts, sometimes aggressively, at other times by political intrigue and subversion. It is perhaps significant, however, that even in the so-called "neutralist" countries that maintain relations with the Communist bloc and receive aid from them, the Communists have from time to time met with sharp rebuffs.

The interest of the United States in this area is recent and for the most part stems from developments growing out of World War II. But the not inconsiderable aid we have given these countries has been marred by instances of inefficient planning, waste of funds, poorly selected personnel and overemphasis on cold war issues and objectives which have given rise to doubts and suspicions among the Asians, many of whom feel that we think of them not as friends and equals but as pawns in the cold war.

For these young nations to have survived in the face of such severe international tensions and such a multitude of difficult problems and to have made even limited progress is, in my opinion, an impressive achievement. Therefore, the picture is not entirely somber. We have helped in the past and can in the future, but this can best be initiated by convincing the people of our sincere friendship. To accomplish this, we need not only intelligent diplomacy, but also much greater understanding and comprehension of our Asian friends as people. To this end this volume by Stanley Karnow and the Editors of LIFE is dedicated.

EDWIN F. STANTON
former U.S. Ambassador to Thailand

A group of field hands (top) cultivates young rice plants in a contoured series of paddies on the island of Sumatra. Rice paddies are kept

submerged in several inches of water during the growing period.

1

A Mosaic of Many Peoples

THE weekly market at Pindaya is a crowded, bustling, chromatic confusion of peoples. In a shaded stall, a Burmese crone squats behind her pyramid of pots and pans and imported steel knives, chewing on a cheroot and politely bargaining with a taciturn Shan farmer in baggy, ankle-length pants and a turkish-towel turban. Nearby, a group of Mongoloid maidens sheathed in shapeless black homespun, their thick calves adorned with brass hoops, giggle timidly as a Chinese stands before an array of mystical charts and hawks his strange medicinal herbs. Along dusty, sunlit alleys, crouching hill women from a dozen separate tribes—each distinguished by bead ornaments or tasseled caps—offer melons, greens, tea leaves and gnarled, esoteric roots to the shifting kaleidoscope of faces, figures and costumes, all so varied, each so singular.

Set in a gentle valley of eastern Burma, this scene is only a single social speck. A hundred miles away in any direction, at another village

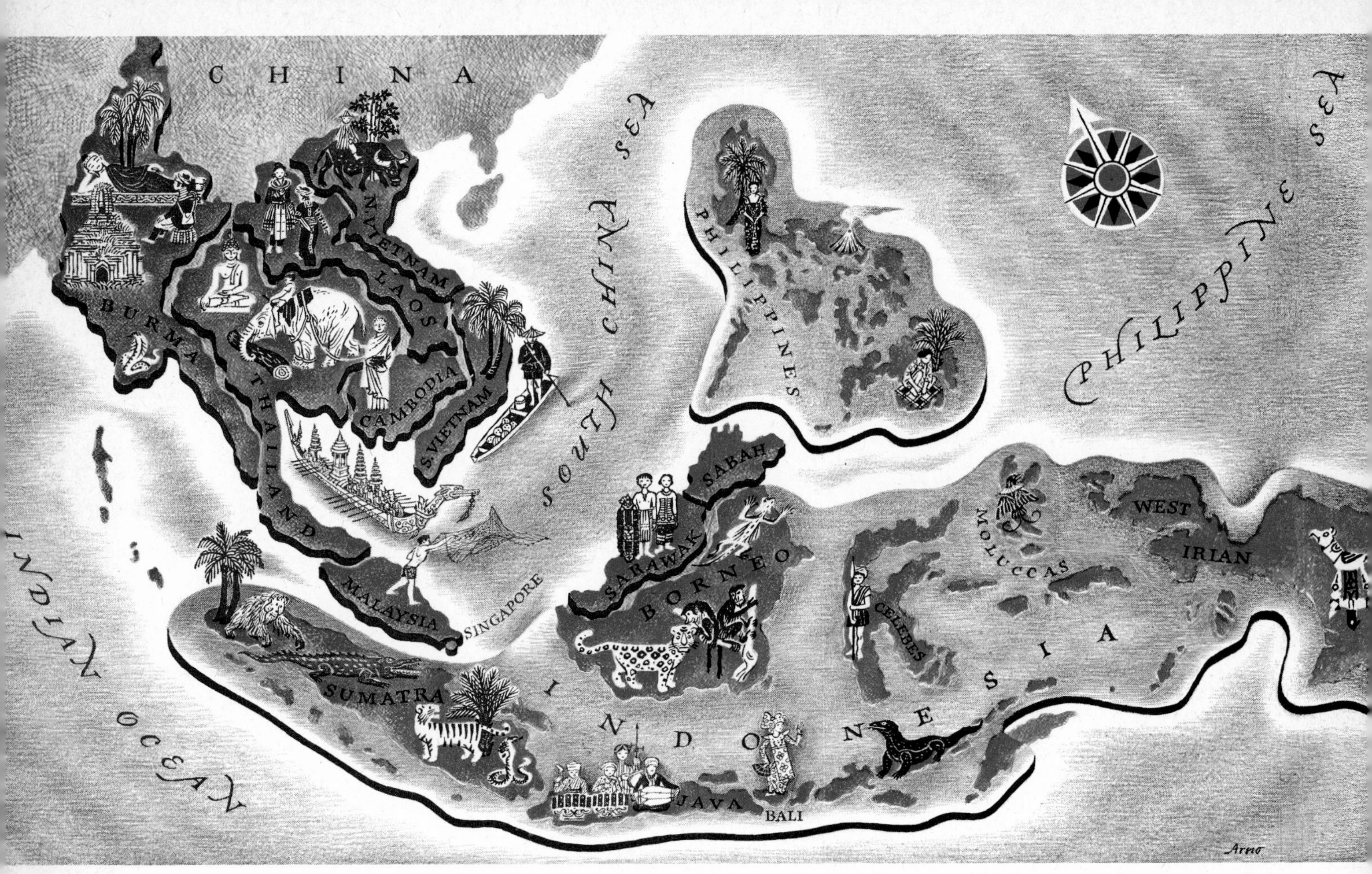

DISCONNECTED COUNTRIES of Southeast Asia, together with some of the familiar or notable characteristics of each, appear above as if they were part of a huge jigsaw puzzle. The state of Malaysia, which came into being in 1963, comprises also the former British colonies of Sarawak and Sabah, formerly known as North Borneo.

market, there is a different assortment of peoples, in different dress, speaking somewhat differently. Visualize these intermingled communities spread over a region half as large as Europe, with a population larger than that of the United States, and a basic reality of Southeast Asia emerges: a vast ethnic mosaic, an anthropologist's paradise. Indeed, as anthropologist Cora Du Bois submits, "There is probably no other area of the world so richly endowed with diverse cultural strains."

The complex human fabric of Southeast Asia is a source of its enigmatic charm, its constant excitement—and the romantic images flicker past, as if in some endlessly fascinating film. Here are orange-robed Buddhist monks, begging bowls in hand, filing beneath the serpentine eaves of a gaudy Bangkok temple. There among the wild orchids and towering trees of a Laotian mountain jungle go Meo hunters, stalking deer and wild boar with primitive flintlocks. A lissome Vietnamese girl in billowing silk pantaloons, her black hair cascading to her waist, cycles down a Saigon boulevard; a Royal Khmer dancer, performing amid the great stone faces of Angkor, pantomimes a Hindu myth as ancient as Athens. Withered Chinese suck opium pipes in a clandestine Singapore den; an Irrawaddy peasant bends over his flooded paddy field, muttering a propitiatory prayer to the *nat,* the ethereal guardian of the rice. Naked Thai boys frolic in a muddy canal the color of themselves; a Malay fisherman gathers in his nets, oblivious to the riotous sunset beyond a palm-studded horizon. On a lawn in Bogor, Javanese musicians sit by a banyan tree, the tinkling of their gamelan orchestra wafting forth with the ambiguity of curling smoke. On and on the images unfold, even as Joseph Conrad observed them: "Brown, bronze, yellow faces, the black eyes, the glitter, the color of an Eastern crowd . . . so old, so mysterious, resplendent and somber."

STRETCHING some 3,800 miles from the western border of Burma through western New Guinea, Southeast Asia is a unified region in name only. It is a convenient geographical label that was popularized to cover Lord Louis Mountbatten's command during World War II, and it describes a corner of the world that is neither a political nor a cultural entity. Except for Thailand, which curiously escaped colonial rule, each of its states is newly independent; all are self-consciously groping for some measure of internal unity. And there is scarcely any common denominator for the area as a whole. Unlike the nations of Europe, Southeast Asia's states have few commercial dealings with one another; unlike the lands of Latin America, they do not intimately share history, language or religion; and even unlike Africans, Southeast Asians lack any feeling quite comparable to the intangible, subjective sentiment that President Léopold Senghor of the West African republic of Senegal has called *négritude.*

Southeast Asia's geography is as balkanized as its peoples. The continental countries of Burma, Thailand, Laos, Cambodia and a politically divided Vietnam are a dispersion of broad plains, wide plateaus and tiny valleys set among hills and mountain ranges whose peaks reach up to 19,000 feet. This is the region of the great rivers—the Mekong, the Chao Phraya and the Irrawaddy—which plunge down from Tibet or southern China and splay out into fertile, rice-growing deltas as they reach the sea. These are lands of jungles, all ablaze with wild poinsettias, frangipani and rhododendrons, and rich in sandalwood and teak. Here are tigers, langurs and the sacred white elephant; and in the highlands wander primeval tribes like the Rhadé or Jarai of Vietnam, said in legend to be men with tails, or the vanishing Yumbris, so rare and elusive that the Thais consider them phantoms and call them *Phi Tong Luang,* Spirits of the Yellow Leaves.

Separated from the mainland by shallow seas —which in recent geological time were land— insular Southeast Asia is a huge archipelago whose capriciously strewn islands stretch far out into the Pacific. Some 7,000 form the Philippines; about 3,000 comprise Indonesia; and the Malay Peninsula, an island *manqué,* may someday be severed from the continent of Asia by the projected Kra Isthmus canal. Here is Columbus' unattained goal, the fabled Spice Islands—Buru, Ceram, Halmahera and Morotai—where Sinbad the Sailor found peppers, cloves, cinnamon, pearl divers, cannibal kings and savages who "know not prayer nor call to prayer."

THE wealth of these places long has obsessed oil prospectors, rubber planters and copra merchants; and as they have for 2,000 years, Chinese traders still ply the island coasts for tasty birds' nests and crocodile skins. Borneo's jungles contain scarce birds and beasts like the orangutan, the proboscis monkey and the double-horned rhinoceros; the tangled forests are also the home of the Dyaks, once headhunting "wild men" but now tamed.

For centuries, Southeast Asia has been a receptive area, ingesting a slow, relentless flow of outside peoples and influences. Migrant races seeking new soil or peaceful surroundings pushed into the region from China, and throughout the centuries many were harassed or subjected by Chinese military and political powers forever contemptuous of the *Nan-Man,* or "southern barbarians." Contrastingly peaceful in its approach to the area, India spread religion and culture from which sprang the roots of much Southeast Asian thought, civilization and art.

Except in Bali, where they still flourish, the Hindu cults brought from India faded. But Buddhism, which like Christianity thrived far from its birthplace, remains vigorously alive throughout Burma, Thailand, Cambodia, Laos and Vietnam. And its emphasis on moderation, justice, patience and kindness, its essentially human yet transcendental qualities are revealing clues to behavior in parts of Southeast Asia. The unworldliness of Buddhism may explain, for example, the disarming candor of a Burmese government leader. Its pacifism is reflected by Laotian soldiers when they purposely shoot over their enemies' heads. What may often seem to be indolence or inertia is, in large measure, inbred passivity. The West puts a premium on action but in the East, as a religious scholar suggested, "the passionless sage is still in popular esteem superior to warriors, statesmen and scientists."

INDIAN Moslem merchants from Gujerat and Bengal also brought Islam to Southeast Asia, and the creed adapted itself to the new environment. It syncretized with earlier Brahmanism and Buddhism or fused with local mysticism; and it is an Islam that few Arabs would recognize. Except for the Darul Islam insurgents of Java and other fanatic bands elsewhere in Indonesia, most of whom agitate hopelessly for a theocratic state, Indonesian Moslems are tolerant, unorthodox and almost casual about religion. In Malaysia as well, it appears more a formality than a fervent faith. The coffee-colored speaker of parliament seems to show more reverence for his ceremonial wig and mace than for the Moslem prayer he intones at each session.

Islam's sweep into Southeast Asia in the 14th and 15th Centuries was, in part, the catalyst that aroused the West's interest in the area. After the Moors had been driven from Europe, the Portuguese set out upon another crusade to destroy them in Asia—and, while they were at it, to seek wealth too.

This was the beginning of a tremendous European impact that continues to this day. It started with adventurers, missionaries and soldiers and with traders searching for gold and spices, and at first it touched the region only lightly. But among other factors, the industrial revolution of the 18th and 19th Centuries, with its vast appetite for raw materials, brought on modern imperialism. Technicians, businessmen, officials and whole armies poured into the Orient, and when the Suez Canal was opened in 1869, their numbers increased.

UNLIKE earlier migrants into Southeast Asia, these most recent arrivals carried with them something unique—a sense of order and administration. This was imposed upon a galaxy of native kingdoms, principalities, city-states, federations and scattered villages. As if they were tracing lines on a patchwork quilt, ignoring where one color began and the other ended, Europe's colonial powers staked out their Far Eastern possessions in a rather arbitrary manner. Seemingly "natural borders," such as rivers and mountains, became borders whether they were genuine ethnic frontiers or not.

Map making of this kind gave Southeast Asia a new kind of fragmentation. It bestowed upon the area that singularly western invention, the national boundary. And within each of the newly defined territories, interests and attachments were canalized away from the Orient to the ruling European mother country. This has resulted, even after independence, in a Southeast Asia that Professor George McTurnan Kahin compares to a Manhattan apartment building: the tenants occupy adjoining flats but rarely speak to each other, and their friends are elsewhere.

Prince Sihanouk of Cambodia often travels to Paris, Peking, Moscow and New York; but as his country's leader he has made only one trip to Saigon, capital of next-door South Vietnam, and has not returned since. The late Prime Minister Marshal Sarit Thanarat of Thailand and Prime Minister General Ne Win of Burma, neighbors in Asia, did not meet until 1958, and then only by accident; they were both patients at the Walter Reed Hospital in Washington. For every Filipino who visits Saigon or Kuala Lumpur, hundreds go to Rome and New York. Trade relations follow a similar pattern. The same brand of razor blade can be bought in Vientiane, Manila or Rangoon, but each of these cities imports the product from different countries—respectively, France, the United States and England.

Colonialism did more than create new borders and habits. Western techniques and enterprise disrupted traditions and altered ways of life. Modern hygiene and medicine, for example, reduced infant mortality and contributed to the lengthening of life. European business introduced new techniques and commercialized Southeast Asia's resources, and now the region produces nearly 90 per cent of the world's rubber, 75 per cent of its copra, 55 per cent of its palm oil, 50 per cent of its tin and 20 per cent of its tungsten. Inevitably, colonialism was the funnel for new ideas of social humanism and nationalism which, in time, led to independence. And from the West, Asia also first acquired the doctrine that threatens further disruptions—communism.

THE presence of the West, in one form or another, is immediately obvious in Southeast Asia. Much of it is a relic of the imperial past—Amsterdam's canals in the heart of Djakarta, now putrid sewers; the broad, shadeless streets of Rangoon, their Whitehall buildings now stained with mildew; the Edwardian Eastern & Oriental Hotel in Penang, where the ghosts of Somerset Maugham characters seem to emerge from the nut-brown woodwork. But the West's impact is continuing. The roads around cities burgeon with billboard advertising and an occasional television aerial, and nearly every ramshackle Chinese noodle shop has its grand white refrigerator. Sultans and civil servants crowd the golf courses of Kuala Lumpur and Singapore; Manila businessmen, some of them inspired by a Dale Carnegie Institute branch office, are faithful Rotarians, Elks and Lions. Saigon lawyers read Sartre and Robbe-Grillet, and sip Beaujolais with their meals. Even Thailand, never a European possession, has not escaped the trend. Lovely Queen Sirikit is dressed by Balmain; King Bhumibol Adulyadej, born in the suburbs of Boston (while his father was a Harvard student), was educated in Switzerland and plays the jazz clarinet.

Yet western influence may be hardly more than a thin veneer. Widespread as it appears, it affects mostly a small elite, barely touching large numbers of Southeast Asia's population. This has produced startling contrasts. Within the past hundred years, for example, European and Europeanized planters have built up modern estates growing rubber or sugar for export markets; elsewhere in Malaysia, Sumatra and the Philippines, peasants work their subsistence farms just as their ancestors did for a thousand years. Many of them ask for nothing more. Not long ago, a United Nations productivity mission revisited a Laotian village and found it completely dormant. "You showed us how to double our crop last year," the headman explained, "so there's no need for us to work this season. We have enough food."

This sort of "dual economy" is paralleled by a similar cleavage in other realms—in entertainment, music, art. City dwellers have become Doris Day fans and viewers of television westerns; villagers still eagerly await an itinerant storyteller or a traveling company to perform traditional blood-and-thunder episodes of heroic kings and conniving courtiers. In his hot, crowded Singapore rooms, Cheong Soo-pieng paints canvases as abstract as any in Provincetown or Paris; squatting on the floor of an airy, stilted house on the Chao Phraya River below Ayutthaya in central Thailand, a lean rice farmer named Sawet Krataiphuek patiently carves teakwood tables and temple doors with the same ornate designs his great-grandfather followed a century ago.

THE real values of the West have not been deeply digested by Southeast Asian societies. While proclaiming his devotion to modern government, a Laotian leader will blithely compose a cabinet from among his cousins, nephews and brothers, shocking nobody but the callow Westerner unaware of the demands of family relationships. Even a cosmopolitan Philippine senator, expounding civic virtues in his

Independence Day oration, may be up to his ears in graft and corruption—perhaps less out of sheer greed than from profound kinship ties. Almost all of Southeast Asia's states have constitutions based on British, French or American models, complete with guarantees of free speech, press and assembly, judicial responsibility and executive limitations. Yet only the Philippines, Malaysia and Singapore practice recognizable—if somewhat inexpert—democracy. Elsewhere, government is one-man rule.

In everyday parlance, underdeveloped lands are called nations. And most of the countries of Southeast Asia are trying to build something more solid than an artificial pretense of political unity—to create what European states took centuries to achieve: real nationhood. But the process of blending diverse peoples cannot be accomplished overnight, and in some places it may seem impossible. Malaysia is mainly divided between Moslem Malay farmers, most of them poor and uneducated, and wealthier Chinese who live in towns for the most part. Ever since independence, Burma has been plagued by recurrent disorder instigated by rebellious Shans, Karens, Kachins, Mons and Arakanese, and continual military action against them has been costly. Indonesia's official motto, *Bhinneka Tunggal Ika,* or "Unity in Diversity," is more an aspiration than a reality. Various island peoples have skirmished for years against the central government. But former President Sukarno's oratory, combined with his skillful use of such irredentist issues as the claim for West New Guinea, helped him to bring the rebels into his national fold.

THE quest for effective government and solid institutions is a preoccupation in Southeast Asia, and some of the experiments might bewilder the western student of textbook politics. Six of the area's countries—Indonesia, the Philippines, Burma, Singapore, North Vietnam and South Vietnam—call themselves republics. The four others—Thailand, Cambodia, Malaysia and Laos—classify themselves as constitutional monarchies. But these political labels are, for the most part, theoretical. The governments of Southeast Asia are usually what their leaders make them.

Apparently inspired by a visit to Red China in 1957, Indonesia's former President Sukarno rejected western parliamentary practice of debate and opposition which he called "chatterbox democracy . . . not in harmony with the soul of the Indonesian nation." He created a totalitarian system, named "guided democracy," to reinforce his personal leadership. Ousted in 1967, Sukarno was replaced by a military-led regime that continued to term Indonesia a "republic." North Vietnam, the only Communist state in Southeast Asia, is officially styled a "democratic republic." South Vietnam is theoretically a western-type republic. Since the downfall of President Ngo Dinh Diem's dictatorship in 1963, however, it has had a variegated series of civilian and military governments that, like most governments in the region, have been republican in name only.

CAMBODIA is directed by Prince Norodom Sihanouk, a popular young man who has held every key post in the country, including prime minister and king (he abdicated the throne in favor of his father in 1955). He calls himself *Chef d'Etat,* and the state is himself. Thailand is a constitutional monarchy run by a military oligarchy that has been promising for years to promulgate a constitution. Parliamentary democracy under former Premier U Nu failed twice in Burma and has been succeeded by a military government under General Ne Win. But the democratic process seems to function in Malaysia and Singapore; and largely as a result of American concentration on education and law during 50 years of tutelage, the Philippines has a rather reckless representative system described by some observers as a "raw democracy." A sign in the lobby of the Philippine Congress reads: "No firearms allowed inside the session hall."

In an effort to exploit their human resources, most Southeast Asian countries have vigorously expanded their educational facilities and have passed laws making primary schooling mandatory. But adult literacy rates are still low throughout the area, ranging from about 75 per cent in the Philippines to only 15 per cent in Laos. And more extensive education has, in its way, fostered new problems. College and high school standards have dropped. Perhaps more serious, education has created expectations that cannot easily be fulfilled by economies that lack capital and managerial skills, and that have not grown fast enough to keep pace with the demand for skilled employment. Few of the area's countries show promise of long-term economic expansion.

SOUTHEAST ASIA'S internal political, social and economic problems are compounded by an overwhelming external threat: the perilous weight of China hanging to the north. Attitudes of fear and respect towards the Chinese have run continuously through the region's history.

Now under Communist control and striving to become a major world power, China views Southeast Asia as its "sphere of influence." In part, the area's immense natural resources are potential fuel for the modern industries China hopes to build. Before World War II, Southeast Asia exported as much as 6.5 million tons of rice annually, a source of food that China, with its narrow margin of arable land, could use. In part, too, the region may attract China as *lebensraum* because of the latter's huge population, which should reach a billion by the end of the century. To some extent, underpopulated Southeast Asia today resembles the southern Chinese provinces of Yunnan, Kweichow, Szechwan and Kwangtung before they were gradually occupied by the Han Chinese 15 or 20 centuries ago.

Most significantly, however, China's expansionism is ideological. As they have repeatedly stated, the Chinese regard their concept of peasant Communism as a model to be imitated by revolutionary movements in underdeveloped countries throughout the world. In some parts of Southeast Asia, this concept has been promoted by overseas Chinese residents. In most of the area, though, the "national liberation" theme publicized by Peking has been spread by indigenous agents, often without any reference to Communism. Experienced operatives among the hill tribes of Thailand, Laos and Vietnam, for example, have appealed to the mountaineers' atavistic dislike of valley peoples. Other agents have exploited the often understandable antipathy of poor peasants for richer city folk. The enormous United States military presence in Vietnam has prompted Communist insurgents there to evoke nationalism.

In their characteristically fragmented fashion, the states of Southeast Asia contend with Communist danger in different ways. Some, like the Philippines, Thailand and South Vietnam, have placed themselves under American protection. Other countries behave more equivocally.

Cambodia's Prince Sihanouk, for example, privately believes that China will eventually dominate the entire region. He has tried to accommodate himself to the future by keeping on good terms with Peking while protecting his country's national sovereignty. But the "Great Proletarian Cultural Revolution," Communist leader Mao Tse-tung's reckless drive to purify China, has stimulated overseas Chinese communities in Southeast Asia to political action of their own. Thus Sihanouk's ties with Peking have become increasingly strained as he strives to resist what he has called "extraordinary interference" by the Chinese in his domestic affairs.

BUT communism's most serious threat lies less in its subversion or its propaganda than in its chance of capitalizing on poverty, passivity, fractionalism, ethnic rivalries, social tensions, ignorance, economic stagnation and political instability. All these are Communist trump cards in the region. For, unfortunately, such weaknesses characterize many lands of Southeast Asia—countries that have been catapulted into the contemporary world with scant preparation in their past to solve present predicaments or to meet future pressures.

AWE-STRUCK, two Burmese girls *(left)* gaze raptly at a painting of episodes in the life of the Buddha in a chapel of Rangoon's Shwe Dagon Pagoda, which contains *(background)* a fine gilded statue of a reclining Buddha.

GEMLIKE in their brilliantly colored blouses, a procession of Balinese women *(opposite)* marches down a jungle path, the baskets balanced on their heads filled with offerings of food and fruit which will be blessed at a nearby temple.

A Changing Area's Brilliant Contrasts

Despite all the complexities and muddles of life in Southeast Asia, there emerges a breathtaking beauty, one often born of the region's very contradictions. The old cities pulse with modern life while serving as a backdrop for brilliant, ancient ceremonies. Weirdly mixed creeds and cultures have produced arts and customs at once intricate and serenely impressive. Even poverty and strife, in a setting of sun, sea and jungle, sometimes seem to lose their horror.

RUBBER TREES in endless rows cast a cathedral pall over a plantation in western Malaysia. During the early morning hours, women tappers collect latex from the tall trunks. Throughout the 19th Century, most raw rubber came from South America, where the tree *Hevea brasiliensis* grows wild. But as world demand increased,

British botanists brought the tree to the East Indies, where with cheap labor and a favorable soil and climate they cultivated it on vast plantations. Today, the Federation of Malaysia stands heir to the phenomenal success of this horticultural transplant and primarily for that reason is the most prosperous nation in Southeast Asia.

DELIGHTED CHILD takes a deep sniff of the flowers she and a friend have picked in one of the forests of Bali. They will weave the flowers into a garland to offer at their Hindu temple.

ELABORATE TERRACES of growing rice dwarf the Balinese field workers who cultivate them by hand with meticulous care. The paddies are irrigated with a network of dams and sluices.

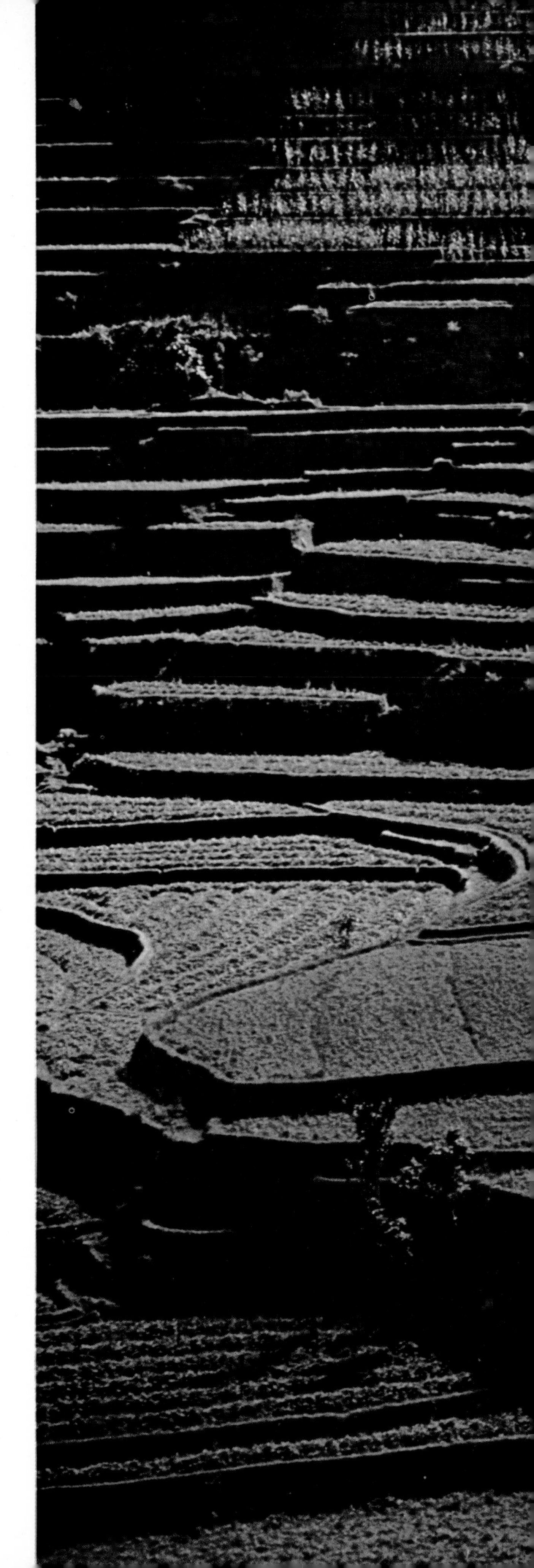

MODERN TECHNOLOGY, still rare in the countryside, has invaded the big cities, where innovations such as movie theaters, gas stations and playgrounds are an integral part of daily life

MOVIE-GOERS, indulging a favorite pastime, line up beneath a giant poster in downtown Bangkok. Though the Thais make some of their own films, most are imported.

LAVISH POOLS near Manila are government-run. The recreation project, a model of its kind, reflects a growing concern in the Philippines for the welfare of the public.

KING'S FUNERAL in Laos comes to a climax as the crematory fire under the gilded coffin begins to blaze. Subjects of King Sisavang Vong, who died in 1959, ascend the steps to the ornate pyre to add sticks to the fire.

RELIGIOUS FESTIVAL celebrating the end of Buddhist Lent draws crowds of worshipers with floral offerings to the high, columned stairway of the Shwe Dagon Pagoda, an immense Buddhist temple in Rangoon, Burma.

A giant Buddha, its stone mottled by age, gazes serenely across the tops of a few of the many shrines that make up the immense Buddhist

temple of Borobudur, built in central Java during the Eighth Century.

2

The Limitless Horizon

WHEN a Thai or Vietnamese farmer is asked where his people originated, he is apt to reply that they have "always lived in this village" because he can, after all, remember his grandfather. Throughout Southeast Asia, tradition may be supreme, but chronological time has little meaning. Early Chinese and European travelers who roamed the region kept careful chronicles—now important sources for western scholars—but the native peoples themselves were indifferent to history. What they knew or cared about the past came down to them not in any systematic account of events, but in myths and legends that were, to their ears, just awesome or charming literary magic.

In the Philippines, for example, local raconteurs tell of a time when all that existed in the world were the sea, the sky and a flying bird. Wearied by its constant flight and having no place to land, the bird cleverly provoked a quarrel between the sea and the sky. The sea threw huge, foaming waves against the sky, which retaliated by hurling massive boulders into the sea—and these first islands on earth were the Philippines.

Archeologists and anthropologists may try to unravel the origin of Laos' hodgepodge of peoples, but troubadours who thread their way through the villages of the Mekong River valley know the answer. They sing of an ancient chieftain whose buffalo died, and from the animal's nostrils sprang a vine that bore three pumpkins. When the pumpkins ripened, something seemed to stir inside them. The chieftain pierced them with a hot iron, and streams of men poured forth—so many that he cut new openings with a knife to let out more. Those who emerged from the burned holes were charred, and from them descended the dark Malay-type peoples called Khas; those who came through the cleaner exits are the lighter, more Mongoloid Lao peoples.

But science too can offer poetic tales of mankind in Southeast Asia. The region's navigable rivers, accessible valleys and land bridges made it an area without dead ends. Its surrounding waters—the South China and Java Seas and the Gulf of Siam—formed a virtual inland sea as familiar as the Mediterranean, and as much an avenue for movement. Here the horizon was not a limitation but an invitation to push forward, perhaps down the Salween River from Tibet, or through Yunnanese mountain gaps to Laos and Vietnam, or over island steppingstones from Malaya into Indonesia and on to Australia. No matter where one chooses to stand in Southeast Asia—as a historian once put it—one can assume that something has gone before and something will follow.

MAN can trace his ancestry in these lands half a million years—back to his own precursor, *Pithecanthropus erectus,* or Java man, whose fossilized skulls have been discovered on the banks of the Solo River and elsewhere in Java. But not until ages later did broadly defined human groups appear in the region. Their precise origin is still a subject of much speculation. Anthropologists think that most of these peoples came from southern China or central Asia and wandered slowly, relentlessly southward over the centuries.

Many migrants probably moved before the melting glaciers of the last ice age raised the sea level, thereby separating from the continent the present-day islands of Indonesia and the Philippines. There were Australoid types, much like contemporary Australian aborigines; and cinnamon-colored, flat-nosed Veddoids, perhaps of African antecedents, whose traces remain in parts of Indonesia, Ceylon and southern India. There were passages of other peoples en route to Pacific islands, among them the Negritos, whose heirs still survive in the Philippines, Malaya and Indonesia. Now almost extinct, those in Malaya—called Semang—live much as they did millennia ago, sleeping in rock or tree shelters, propitiating the kindly elves of jungle flowers, and appeasing thunderstorms by cutting their shins and offering blood.

THE last of the prehistoric migrations, dating back some 4,500 years, brought in Malay-type peoples variously called Austronesians or Indonesians or Deutero-Malays and Proto-Malays. Their descendants, now intermixed with many other ethnic strains, form the basic population of Southeast Asia. These people developed the technique of rice cultivation in irrigated paddy fields, on terraced hillsides or in the fertile ashes of burned forests. They learned to raise pigs and chickens and to grow fruit and vegetables. These agricultural innovations were momentous, for they transformed nomadic hunters into settled farmers.

Out of this new stability evolved village communities with many of the spiritual rites and social customs that, passed down by word of mouth, are still observed. The clumsy water buffalo was domesticated, to become the ubiquitous beast of burden throughout Southeast Asia. Animist beliefs in the forces of nature developed, so strongly that they persistently flourish today beneath the crust of more formal religions. When the art of using bronze reached Southeast Asia from China, primitive

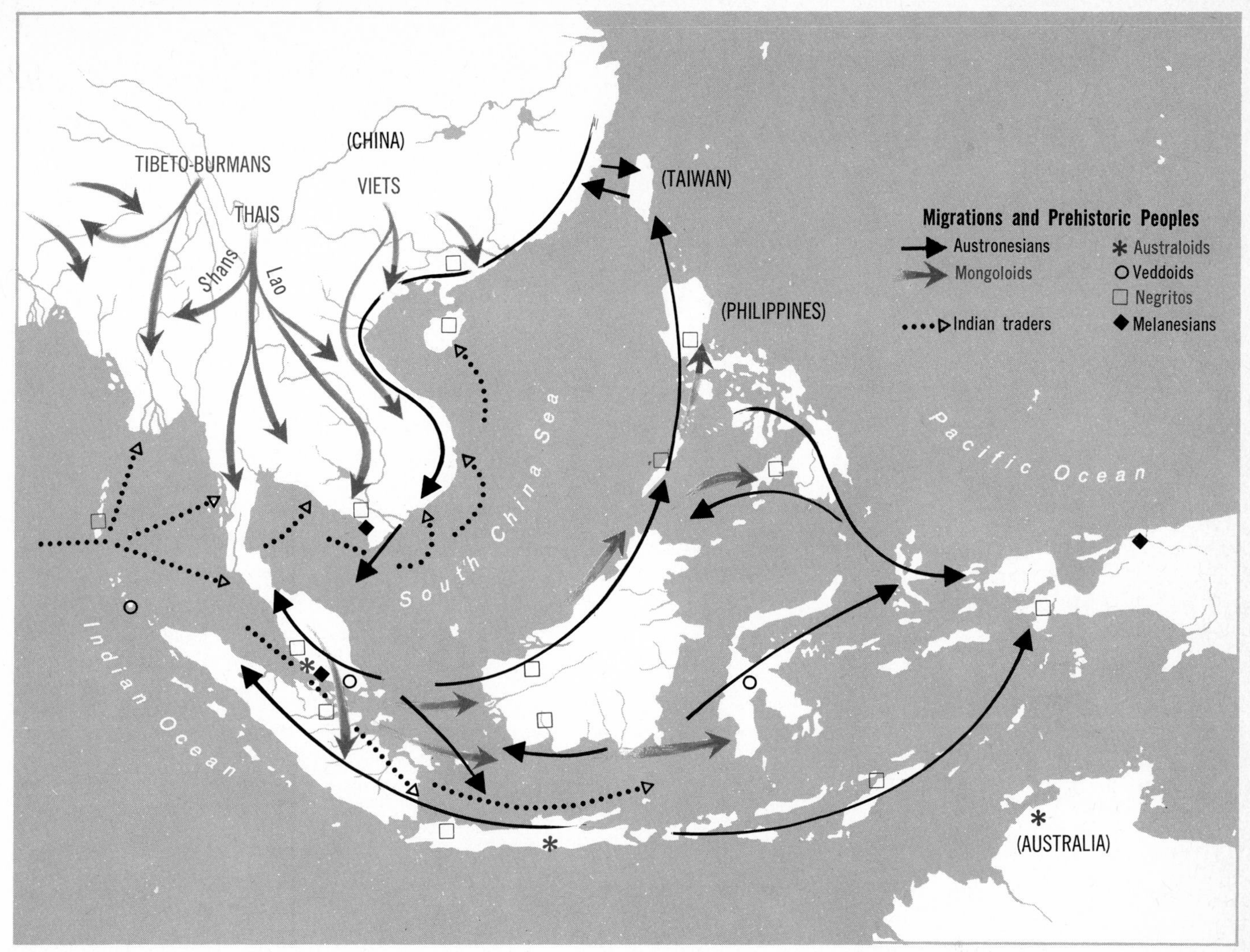

RECEPTIVE REGION, Southeast Asia has been traversed by waves of peoples, starting as early as 10,000 to 8000 B.C. Routes of the four earliest groups are not known, but their descendants or artifacts have been found in the locations shown. The paths of the last two groups, the Austronesians and Mongoloids, are indicated by arrows.

craftsmen fashioned large ritual drums adorned with frogs and elephants, which Bangkok antique dealers now sell to affluent western ladies as cocktail tables.

These settlers were never to live undisturbed. Just as they had absorbed or destroyed earlier peoples, so fresh floods of migrants followed in their wake. Many of these "migrations" were, in reality, conquests by warriors who carved out new kingdoms and imposed their culture on the defeated inhabitants of an area. Or, as often occurred, the conquerors took over the rich valleys, scattering their victims into the hills. Indeed, some present mountain tribes are peoples who never recovered from past invasions, and a significant theme in current Southeast Asian folklore is the constant struggle between highlanders and lowlanders.

Frequently the invaders themselves were in their turn beaten, absorbed or forced to move by new intruders. When Mongoloid Viet tribes wandered south from China about 200 B.C., they found aboriginal Malay inhabitants whom they absorbed, destroyed or drove into the hills. But hardly had these migrants adapted to their new home in Vietnam when stronger forces came down from the north. The extraordinary Han Chinese, their power consolidated in the Yellow River valley, had sent cavalry forth to expand their empire. They annexed Vietnam in 111 B.C., and a century later the Chinese began to infuse the Vietnamese aristocracy with their literature, their political concepts and the ethics of Confucius and Buddhism. The Vietnamese regained their independence nearly a thousand years afterward, but their culture has remained strongly Sinicized ever since.

With variations, there were similar patterns of movement in other corners of Southeast Asia. Amid all the turbulent, labyrinthic confusion of migrations and wars, perhaps no people were more adaptable than the Thais. Legend has it that Thai nomads trekked from central Asia into southern China about 2000 B.C. and eventually founded small states along the Yangtze River from Szechwan province to the sea. But ultimately they also felt pressure from the Chinese to the north. Some Thai tribes, each led by its *chao* (chieftain), wandered south to form postage-stamp-sized principalities called *muongs* in the present countries of Laos, Burma and Thailand. Others accepted imperial suzerainty, married their women to Chinese warriors and, as many peoples of Asia would later do, obeyed the Chinese dictum—"Yours to pay tribute, mine to bestow rank."

SEVERAL Thai tribes resisted, however, and about the middle of the Seventh Century A.D. these groups—mixed with other peoples—created the Kingdom of Nanchao in the area of southern China. Based on a narrow plain hugging a lake more than 6,000 feet up in the Yunnan mountains, these Thais—whose name means "free"—maintained their independence for centuries. Sometimes they defeated invading Chinese; often they went off to ravage areas as distant as Vietnam. Some students of this tumultuous epoch suggest that if the Thais had operated from a broader economic base, they might have succeeded in overthrowing the emperors of China. Amid these recurrent wars, however, the Thais gradually absorbed elements of Chinese culture by intermarriage and by kidnaping or hiring Chinese artisans and scholars.

This cultural symbiosis had two effects: it slowly brought Chinese civilization farther to the south, and it greatly Sinicized the Thais, who were already beginning to migrate into Southeast Asia. Their flight south gathered momentum in the 13th Century. By this time, however, they had been weakened by internecine squabbles, and they were easy prey for Kublai Khan's Mongols, who so devastated the tribal regions that, as Marco Polo noted later, they "cannot be reoccupied and barely traveled through."

OVER the centuries, Chinese pressures on the "southern barbarians" tightened or loosened, depending on the whims and fortunes of China's Heavenly Emperors. But at one time or another almost every state in Southeast Asia was forced or persuaded to pay tribute to China, and some volunteered gifts in exchange for Chinese military protection. During the brief but destructive rule of the Mongols over China, Chinese excursions into the region were outright invasions or punitive expeditions. At later times, China more subtly extended its influence over lands of the area, cajoling or flattering native leaders with displays of pomp and pageantry and extravagant sojourns at the imperial court—much as the present Peking regime pursues its public relations.

Chinese activities in Southeast Asia were almost wholly political, and sometimes belligerent. By contrast, India during the same period peacefully exerted a far more profound cultural and religious influence in the region. Hindu and Buddhist legends testify to ties between India and Southeast Asia that go back thousands of years. Hardy sailors for centuries had explored the seas between the two regions. Yet it was not until the start of the Christian era that the Indians began to push vigorously toward the area.

The reasons for this dynamic expansion are not entirely clear. Perhaps it was caused by the proselytizing zeal of Buddhism, which had shucked off the caste barriers imposed by Hinduism and did not fear the contamination of contact with alien barbarians. But most likely the immediate motive behind this new momentum was largely material. India's gold supplies, traditionally imported from Siberia, had been cut off when nomadic movements in central Asia endangered caravan routes and when efforts to buy precious metals from Rome proved unsuccessful. Thus the Indians reoriented their commerce toward Southeast Asia, long known in Sanskrit lore as *Suvarnadvipa* and *Suvarnabhumi,* the islands or lands of gold.

Technical progress at the time favored this switch in tactics. Contemporary builders of merchant fleets had learned to construct large, seagoing junks. About the same time, the Greek pilot Hippalus had discovered the secret of using the monsoon's seasonal winds, a key to travel until then known in the West only to the Arabs. Not long afterward, in the Second Century, a Greco-Roman geographer named Claudius Ptolemy published a remarkably accurate annotated atlas describing places as remote as Borneo. This information must have come to him directly or indirectly from the Indian traders.

CASTING off from ports along the Coromandel Coast, Indian vessels were swept by southwesterly summer winds across the Bay of Bengal to Burma and the Malay Peninsula, through the Straits of Malacca to Sumatra and Java, or around Singapore to the present sites of Thailand, Cambodia and Vietnam.

As the Indian ships reached an unknown shore, their captains would meet the native chiefs, distribute gifts and care for the sick. It was essential for the intruder in primitive lands to appear both wealthy and possessed of magical power, and once this was demonstrated, he would contrive to marry the chief's daughter. As an aristocrat, she was then the ideal instrument for propagating her husband's religion and customs. Without much additional strain, she could also promote his business interests. Unlike the Chinese and Europeans, the Indians never demanded territory or tribute in the name of a foreign kingdom, and they dealt with these pristine tribesmen as equals.

In a happy meeting of cultural supply and demand, the various native peoples were receptive to Indian contributions. They first copied Indian concepts, then adapted them to their own environment. In the millennium to follow, there was a heady efflorescence of Indian influence throughout Southeast Asia.

In many areas Indian advisers taught the people to irrigate and drain their soil, to build canals and port cities. Indian religion, with its hold on all facets of life, gave local kings a divine status, a role of both god and high priest. These imported beliefs were synthesized with ancient animistic reverence for the forces of nature, and out of this mystical marriage were born distinctive new civilizations.

The first known of these Indianized states, Funan, was established in the present area of Cambodia about the First Century A.D. Funan died, but it passed on a pattern of experience that, in the hands of greater genius, led to more dazzling kingdoms. The Sailendra Dynasty, which rose in Java in the Seventh Century, eventually extended its dominion over most of insular Southeast Asia. Even more impressive was the Cambodian kingdom of Angkor, whose reconstructed temples still remain one of the world's wonders.

Elsewhere in Southeast Asia similar states mushroomed, all showing some degree of Indian inspiration in their art, religion and government. Seagoing Champa, which rose on the coast of central Vietnam, constructed prodigious Brahmanic and Buddhist temples, most of them now lost to the jungles. There were Indianized settlements in Malaya, and the Buddhist Mons founded kingdoms in southern Thailand and Lower Burma. In the islands of Indonesia, maritime empires spiraled to dizzy heights of power and then crumbled, and new states emerged from their ruins.

THE Kingdom of Srivijaya, for example, grew during the Sixth Century under Buddhist auspices in the southern Sumatran river port of Palembang, now an ugly city of oil refineries and molding office buildings. It was strategically situated near the entrance to the Java Sea, and only about a hundred years after the kingdom's foundation Srivijayan power extended through Sumatra and most of Malaya, western Java and as far as the Philippines.

Buddhist pilgrims often stopped at Srivijaya on their travels between India and China, and during one sojourn, a Chinese monk counted "more than a thousand Buddhist priests who are devoted to study and good deeds." External rivalries and internal conflicts tore Srivijaya asunder in the 13th Century, and about this time Marco Polo, unaware that he was passing through a dismembered empire when he visited Sumatra, noted dutifully that "this island has eight kingdoms and eight crowned kings."

The power of these early Southeast Asian potentates was not unlike the hegemony of feudal European kings. The maharaja nominally reigned over a troublesome assortment of petty chieftains, whom he controlled by punitive expeditions and who, on occasion, assembled enough strength to overthrow him. Very likely, ordinary people outside the imperial capitals knew little about the empire they inhabited. They were ruled by their prince, whose relations with the central authority were of no concern to them. This is still true in countries like Laos, where many rural villagers have never heard of their own state.

THE impact of Indian influence did not always penetrate deeply into the lives of common folk. The Brahmanic cults of Shiva and Vishnu were transformed into cults of divine monarchy, observed mainly by the king and his aristocracy. Buddhism, more individualistic and democratic, was potentially a more popular ethic. But only after centuries did Buddhism gather the strength to become, as it is today, a vital force in the area. In its vigor it inspired prodigies of art and architecture that have rarely been equaled since. Yet Indian influence and native customs were always fused in the crucibles of Southeast Asia, to produce new and different cultures.

The Indians exported more than Brahmanism and Buddhism to Southeast Asia. By the 13th Century, Islam had become entrenched in northern India, and under Moslem traders the port of Cambay in Gujerat grew into a thriving hub of trade between Europe, the Middle East and the Orient. Persians, Arabs, Armenians and Turks carried pearls, perfumes, dyes and Venetian glass into Cambay to exchange them for timber, spices, silks, tin and gold brought from Java, Sumatra, Borneo and Malaya by Gujerati merchants. The Indian Moslems—like Hindus and Buddhists before them and Europeans to follow—recognized the advantage of establishing themselves closer to their sources of raw materials. They moved into the islands of Indonesia, and eventually they based their firms in the conveniently located Malayan coastal town of Malacca.

BEFORE long Malacca was a booming, bustling city-state, nominally under the rule of a native sultan but actually dominated by powerful Gujerati merchants. It was colorfully crowded with every species of mankind, ranging from eastern Mediterranean peoples to those from the steppes of northwestern China, and its *quais* and warehouses were piled high with calico cloth, Ming porcelain, Indian opium and plumed birds from the Banda Islands, their feathers destined for Ottoman harems. "Men cannot estimate the wealth of Malacca," wrote a Portuguese visitor, and it was precisely this wealth, personified in Moslem merchants, that made Islam prestigious. Without entirely abandoning their Brahmanic rituals, Buddhist precepts or magical beliefs, the local kings and princes became Moslems. In time, the new faith—with its sermon of man's equality before the one God Allah—filtered down to the common people of insular Southeast Asia. And this tide of Islamic conversion was, soon afterward, to bring the crashing waves of Europe breaking on the shores of the Orient.

But however much Europe was to change the region and whatever the extent of China's chronic threat to the area, more than a thousand years of Indian influence had immeasurable effect. It endowed nearly all of Southeast Asia with religion, doctrine and ethics, and with art, literature, institutions, ideas and wisdom—in short, civilization.

The walls and towers of Angkor Wat, the great 12th Century temple in Cambodia, are reflected in the temple's 660-foot-wide moat.

Glorious Remains of Vanished Empires

In an age when much of Europe was sunk in anarchy, the architects, masons and sculptors of Southeast Asia were building temples that rival the greatest man-made objects anywhere. Most remarkable are the temples of Borobudur and Prambanan in Java, the holy city of Pagan in Burma and the temples of Angkor in Cambodia. Despite the ravages of time, they remain as monuments to the wealth, power and creative energy of the ancient dynasties that built them.

ORNATE FACADE of the Bayon, a temple at Angkor, looms over a band of saffron-robed Buddhist monks. Like nearby Angkor Wat *(previous page)*, the Bayon was built by kings of the Khmer Empire, which flourished in Cambodia as early as the Ninth Century. Overrun by invaders in 1431, Angkor and its temples were

completely enveloped by the jungle until 1907 when French archeologists began uncovering and restoring these architectural masterpieces. Each of the Bayon's towers bears four faces of what is probably the Buddha; all have the same enigmatic smile. The walls are decorated by vigorous carvings of humans, animals and gods.

GRANDEUR of the ancient shrines combines vast scale with intricacy of design

STATELY TEMPLES at Prambanan in Java were built by Hindu kings during the Ninth Century. Behind them looms Merapi, one of Indonesia's 60 active volcanoes.

SMALL PAGODAS of Pagan in Burma dot the fields by the Irrawaddy River. Begun in the 11th Century, the holy city of Pagan still has ruins of some 2,190 shrines.

MOUNTAIN FAMILY of the Rhadé tribe in Vietnam fords a jungle stream. Rhadé women go bare-breasted and the men, who hunt with crossbows, wear loincloths.

RHADE LONG HOUSE, largely made of woven bamboo *(right)*, shelters several families. The mountain tribes, originally Indonesian, have long hated the Vietnamese.

CRUDE KITCHEN WORK occupies a woman of the Menung tribe as she tosses rice in a shallow pan. Thirty-four different tribes live in the interior of Vietnam.

PRIMITIVE PEOPLES of Vietnam, who centuries ago retreated to remote mountain areas, remain untouched by the modern world and its angry armies

In a furious engagement in the late 16th Century, shown in a vivid drawing of the era, Dutch forces struggle to oust the Portuguese from a

strategic outpost on the island of Tidore in the North Moluccas.

3

An Epoch of Disruption

ON a humid day in May 1498, four small ships commanded by the Portuguese explorer Vasco da Gama lowered anchor off the southwest Indian town of Calicut, and a landing party went ashore. The visitors were uncomfortably dressed in doublet and hose, and their banner bore a Cross. Asked what they sought, the Portuguese replied: "Christians and spices."

Thus opened the tumultuous, heroic and rapacious epoch of European expansion into Asia—an era that, in the kinetic power of its impact, was nothing short of revolutionary. Never before in history had man wrought such gigantic change as in these five centuries of discovery, conquest, religious crusade, trade, exploitation and colonization. In often violent ways, whole countries were uncovered, pacified and controlled, and the European thrust inadvertently produced many things—order, education, hygiene and technology. But most of all, the confrontation and collision of East and West dislocated old traditions and ways of life, and set in motion political, economic, social and psychological forces which even today are far from reaching equilibrium. The waves of this shock still reverberate in all the vast multitude of problems that now face Southeast Asia's lands. Nevertheless, they are modern problems; for in its haphazard fashion, the West catapulted Southeast Asia into the contemporary age.

The dynamic drive of the West toward the East did not gather full momentum until the 19th Century, when the mystique of the white man's racial responsibilities sparked the imagination of European imperialists, and the industrial revolution fired the need for raw materials and markets. But an early portent of that vast movement into Asia could have been observed 500 years before, in a Genoa jail.

There languished a Venetian merchant called Marco Polo, captured in one of the chronic wars between Italy's rival city-states, restlessly reminiscing of his past travels. He told tales of Mongol wealth and of Burmese temple spires "covered with gold, a full finger's breadth in thickness." He spoke of an island called Java, rich in pepper, nutmeg, spikenard, galingale and "all the precious spices that can be found in the world." Europe had heard such tales before from seamen back from the Indies who told of shores where "the sands sparkled and glittered with gems and precious ores."

OF all the oriental treasures that spellbound Europeans, the most appealing were the spices which Marco Polo had described—so rare and expensive that they were more than condiments useful for seasoning and essential to the preservation of food; they were status symbols. Indeed, it was spices that first lured Europeans to the East. Europe knew that pepper vines were abundant in Sumatra and Java and that the eastern islands of the Indonesian archipelago were covered with clove and nutmeg trees. But the hostile Moslem rulers who dominated the trade routes to Europe controlled these sources. Clearly, the way to break this strangling heathen monopoly was to circumnavigate Islam's land power in the Middle East and overcome it from behind, in the Orient.

These crass objectives were reinforced by loftier motives, no less strong. The memory of the stalemated Crusades was still fresh, and many a European monarch saw glorious revenge in a new assault on Islam. At the same time, there was an intangible, complex feeling astir. Europe had lately broken out of the orderly, moral confinement of the Middle Ages. Its surplus energies were growing, seeking to break away from the "prison of the Mediterranean."

WITH papal blessings and the fastest ships afloat, the Portuguese led this new, nautical Crusade of faith and commerce. In their armored galleons and light, speedy caravels—perfected by Prince Henry the Navigator—they gained control of the Indian Ocean, captured the enclave of Goa on the Indian mainland itself and moved into Malacca. By the turn of the 16th Century, they owned an empire. Lisbon replaced Venice as Europe's spice center, and Portuguese traders and swashbuckling adventurers fanned out through the Orient. They were a cruel and capricious lot, and they appalled missionaries. Reporting on the behavior of the Portuguese in the Moluccas, St. Francis Xavier wrote that their knowledge was limited to conjugating the verb *rapere,* to steal, and in this they displayed "an amazing capacity for inventing new tenses and participles."

Scarcely a hundred years after its spectacular rise, the Portuguese empire began to crack under the weight of its own avarice, corruption and mismanagement, and strong rivals entered the race for spices and wealth. First came the Dutch and then the English, and the battles were bitter and bloody.

Life could be misery for these adventurers, who rotted with scurvy or died in sea skirmishes. "Where wouldn't they go for pepper!" the novelist Joseph Conrad later wrote in evocation of their memory. "For a bag of pepper they would cut each other's throats without hesitation, and would forswear their souls . . . the bizarre obstinacy of that desire made them defy death in a thousand shapes; the unknown seas, the loathsome . . . diseases; wounds, captivity, hunger, pestilence, and despair. It made them great! By heavens! it made them heroic; and it made them pathetic, too, in their craving for trade with the inflexible death levying its toll on young and old."

When the enfeebled Portuguese collapsed and the English withdrew to their Indian outposts, the ruthless, determined Dutch emerged victorious. The Dutch United East India Company came to monopolize the world's spice supply, and business was good. A pound of cloves, for example, commanded a 2,000 per cent profit in Europe, and in 1654 the company revealed that its gross income had long averaged 2.5 million guilders per year, an immense sum in those days. Even that amount did not slake their thirst, and with more skill yet no less brutality than the Portuguese, the Dutch reached out for greater riches. They paid slave wages to workers but sold them food at exorbitant prices. They repressed uncooperative native chieftains and destroyed "unauthorized" plantations that might threaten their monopoly. And they tirelessly roamed the seas. They sighted Australia and discovered New Zealand, penetrated Laos, gained footholds in Vietnam and tried to oust the Spanish from Manila.

THE lust for adventure and affluence obsessed Europeans of every country. They became pirates, slave traders or mercenaries to native kings, and some of them became "kings" themselves, ruling tiny islands or remote port towns. A wondrous figure among them was Constantine Phaulkon, a Greek innkeeper's son who rose to prominence in the 17th Century as foreign policy adviser to the king of Siam. As his noble rank warranted, he acquired two palaces, European bodyguards, an English secretary called Mr. Bashpool and a handsome Japanese wife known as Dame Golden Horseshoe. Such was Phaulkon's conceit that petitioners were forced to grovel before him in his audience chamber, and so worrisome was his intriguing that some Siamese feared he would turn their country over to a European nation. A xenophobic Siamese general, the Commander of the Royal Elephants, rose in rebellion, deposed the old king and arrested Phaulkon, his wife and his aides. Mr. Bashpool was imprisoned for years with a plank around his neck. Phaulkon, then aged forty, was hacked to pieces. Dame Golden Horseshoe was tortured and jailed, and in an inscrutably oriental manner was later released and made Controller of the Royal Confectionary, an assignment that inspired her to invent the custard cakes that are still popular in Thailand.

AS brave and peripatetic as the European buccaneers and merchants of Southeast Asia—and far more selfless—were the missionaries. They made few converts among Buddhists and Moslems, but they patiently founded schools and hospitals and pursued their charities. One of the most effective of them was a Frenchman, Alexandre de Rhodes, who went to Vietnam early in the 17th Century. His most significant achievement was the perfection of *Quoc Ngu,* a Roman alphabet radically applied to the tonal Vietnamese language, which hitherto had used Chinese ideographs. The *Quoc Ngu* method of writing, now used everywhere in Vietnam, is one of the most durable European contributions to the Orient.

If Christianity made little headway in most of Southeast Asia, it spread widely in the Philippines, which experienced a wholly different sort of European relationship. Unlike the English, Dutch and Portuguese swashbucklers—whose forts and fleets made little contact with Asians—Spanish conquistadors and colonizers went boldly into the countryside. Nothing like the Indianized civilizations established elsewhere in the region had developed in the Philippines where the people were mostly primitive Malay animists. This facilitated Spanish establishment of a feudal administration and of encomiendas, or fiefs, on which Filipinos were put to work as serfs.

It also made proselytizing smoother for the Church, and parish priests were able to circulate among the lowest levels of the population,

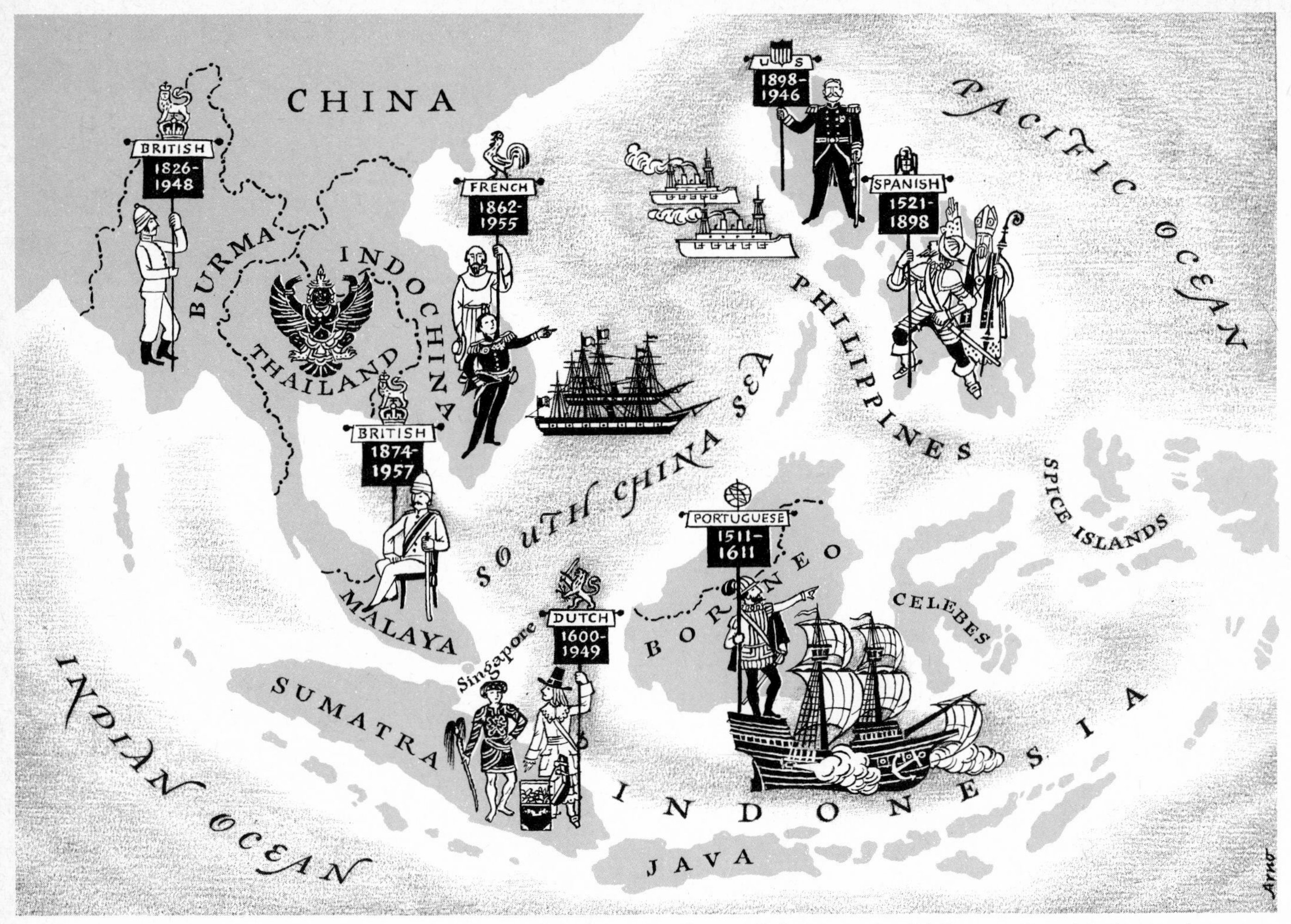

WESTERN COLONISTS held control of almost all of Southeast Asia in recent centuries, as the symbolic figures on the map above illustrate. Not until after World War II, for example, did France relinquish the area known as Indochina, bringing the present-day countries of North and South Vietnam, Laos and Cambodia into existence.

sometimes protecting the natives against harsh landlords and officials. Spanish domination altered Philippine society, such as it was. But if Filipinos were Christianized and Europeanized, their institutions were cast in the rigid, archaic mold of Spain, undeveloped and isolated from the world. Under Spain, as the historian Brian Harrison submits, "the Philippines remained . . . in a state of suspended animation."

Elsewhere in Southeast Asia, however, the faint impulses of impending change were being felt. In Europe the first gears of new industries had turned. The worldwide balance of power shifted as nations pragmatically sought other sources of strength. Self-sufficient, agricultural Britain, for example, was gradually becoming an industrialized country, anxious to import food and raw materials and to find markets overseas for its mass-made cloth. Dutch prosperity in the East had slowly crumbled under the burden of increased overheads and outmoded methods of exploitation, and when the United East India Company was dissolved in 1799, its debts totaled 134 million guilders.

There was also a new, pervasive spirit of enlightenment in the air that inspired fresh trends of colonial thought. Rugged empire builders of the past had referred to Asian princes as "poor, ignorant fools," but now there were Europeans in Batavia and Penang who learned to speak local languages and agitated against slavery. One Dutch official even wrote a didactic poem on the wisdom of Confucius. The most notable child of this liberal movement was an intense, idealistic Englishman named Thomas Stamford Raffles.

The English, attacking Napoleon's allies in the East, had captured Java from the Dutch in 1811, and Raffles had been appointed lieutenant governor. He had instructions to "do all the good we can," and he energetically attempted to reform every aspect of colonial administration. He outlawed torture and abolished the Dutch practice of forcing peasants to deliver quotas of commercial produce. He tried to relegate the hereditary native chiefs to ceremonial symbols, and he instituted a benevolent government to deal with the people directly. He devised an equitable land-rent scheme, which aimed to charge villages rates proportionate to the productivity of their soil.

RAFFLES' reforms were, in short, an ambitious effort to impose western humanitarian ideas and rational techniques on an oriental society, and they did not quite work. For example, he had difficulty accumulating data for calculating rents, and petty native princes refused to abdicate their ancient prerogatives. And even the most reasonable administrative innovations, which required time to mature, threw the government into debt. After five years, Raffles was removed from Java and returned to London. But soon afterward he was back in the Orient, and in 1819 he founded the colony of Singapore, which became one of Britain's most profitable territories.

Despite his lack of success in Java, Raffles contributed significantly to his time. Many of his reforms eventually became normal colonial procedure, and his own scholarly studies of the region were among the first comprehensive works on the subject. More important, he infused western attitudes toward Asia with a new temper. Now Europeans began to consider the presence and often the welfare of the natives, and in response, a certain awareness of the European started to spread among Asians.

This broader contact between East and West coincided after 1850 with a new era of European penetration into Southeast Asia. Contrary to the Communist thesis formulated by Lenin, the imperialism of the late 19th Century was hardly an organized plot of capitalist conspirators, but rather an illogical sequence of movements empirically guided and often ill-directed. Indeed, there was almost a hesitant, fortuitous quality in Europe's conquest of territory.

The British originally invaded Burma because of friction along the Indian border. But their full occupation of the region by 1886 was provoked by the fear that the French might move in instead. It was mainly a desire to salvage national pride after their defeat by Prussia in 1871 that motivated the French to push into Indochina. And despite all the jingoism that accompanied the defeat of the Spanish in Manila Bay by Admiral George Dewey of the United States, many prominent U.S. officials had serious misgivings about grabbing the Philippines from Spain. His hand forced by events, President McKinley somewhat mournfully confessed: "The truth is I didn't want the Philippines and when they came to us as a gift from the gods . . . there was nothing left for us to do but to take them all, and to educate the Filipinos . . . and by God's grace do the best we could do for them."

ONCE installed in Southeast Asia, however, these new imperialists behaved differently from their predecessors. Traders of the past had, with their stockades and sailing fleets, concentrated entirely on commerce. They conquered a land, excluded other nations, bought commodities—usually through the intermediary of a native prince—and carried their bounty back to the mother country for sale. But now, with capitalism in Europe reaching its height, colonies became regions for investment. This meant large plantations, railroads, bridges, roads and complex governmental mechanisms. As Europeans could not possibly conduct these operations alone, some natives began to be educated in basic technical and administrative skills. From among these European-trained people were to come the local nationalist leaders. Europe's large-scale colonial exploitation also introduced new crops and industries, as well as public health measures which in time resulted in a single startling statistic: Southeast Asia's population has increased twentyfold in the past century and a half.

In all this vast change, as in territorial conquests, there was no master plan. Not only did the western nations vary widely in their conduct, but the same powers altered their behavior in different places. "No wise man has a Policy," says one of Rudyard Kipling's fictitious British officials. "A Policy is the blackmail levied on the Fool by the Unforeseen."

The exigencies of European diplomacy following the Napoleonic wars restored the Indonesian islands to the Dutch. At first, the Dutch vacillated in their colonial conduct. They tried briefly to carry on Raffles' liberal program, but the prospects of greater profit swung them to a new policy called the Culture System. In principle, this required each peasant to grow commercial crops for the government on only a fraction of his land. In practice, as the Dutch historian B.H.M. Vlekke has written, "it resulted in the exploitation of Java as though it were one huge plantation owned by the government." Peasants were held accountable for crop failures and forced into labor gangs. The stress on export commodities—coffee, sugar, indigo, pepper and other produce—reduced the acreage available for cultivation of basic foods, causing famine in some areas.

GRADUALLY the Dutch came around to a pattern of paternalistic, indirect rule in Indonesia. Native princes and sultans governed the people, and a network of Dutch officials guided the native chieftains. The Dutch, of course, had the real power, but the average Indonesian peasant was never certain where the authority lay. No clear standards of political conduct were ever formulated, and this kind of vagueness remains today in independent Indonesia, whose governmental structure is probably the weakest in Southeast Asia.

As it did in its other colonies, France approached Indochina with a theoretical *mission civilisatrice* designed to transform natives into Frenchmen. The appeal of Gallic culture was irresistible, and among the Vietnamese are some of the most westernized people in Southeast Asia. But this French ideal was not followed through in practice. Educated Vietnamese were not welcomed into the colonial civil service, and their efforts in private business were blocked by French interests. At the same time, French rule burdened Vietnamese peasants with severe hardships.

RIGIDLY, almost anachronistically protectionist, the French functioned on the principle, as an official report put it, that "colonial production must be limited to supplying the mother country with raw materials and with noncompetitive products." In the rich Mekong River valley, new land was cleared and put to work, and rice output increased enormously. Equally spectacular were the economic contrasts this engendered. French colonists or wealthy Vietnamese acquired vast estates, while three out of four peasants remained tenant farmers, paying 50 or as much as 100 per cent interest on their loans and sliding deeper and deeper into debt. In the higher plateau districts of South Vietnam, French rubber planters requisitioned native workers among the hill people, and as recently as 1950, a French official in the area told the English writer Norman Lewis that if it were not for governmental control the planters would "go into the villages after labor and bring the men back at the point of a gun." Significantly, the Communists made their easiest inroads into these regions.

By curious contrast, economic liberalism also caused upsetting problems. As the British penetrated Lower Burma in the mid-19th Century, they began to encourage rice cultivation in the Irrawaddy River delta, and peasants could have land for the asking. Thousands of peasants poured into the delta region, and millions of acres of paddy land spread out across the hot, humid plain.

But the land in itself is not enough for a farmer. The peasants needed capital for seeds and equipment, and because they lacked any public credit facilities they turned to Chettyar moneylenders, Indian bankers who cheerfully accepted the rice fields as collateral. Unaccustomed to such financial sophistication, the peasants borrowed freely, with predictable results. By 1929 Chettyar investments in Burma were four times the value of British holdings, and a decade later moneylenders owned half of Lower Burma's 10 million acres of farmland.

The British also committed the political error in Burma of using Indians in the most important civil service posts because the practice was "cheaper and easier." But unlike either the Dutch or French, who could not conceive of self-government for their colonies, the British created a legislative council in which elected Burmese began to experience some of the responsibilities of autonomy.

ALWAYS outside the mainstream of Southeast Asian events, the Philippines went through a different evolution. There the United States took over a country that had been more deeply Europeanized by the Spanish, and even before American control was consolidated, the principle of eventual self-government of the islands was recognized. This was reaffirmed in 1907 when President Theodore Roosevelt wrote: "If they handle themselves wisely . . . we shall at the earliest possible moment give them a nearly complete independence."

In preparation for this independence, the United States actuated an intensive program of education. Within less than a generation, the number of high school students in the Philippines increased to nearly 50,000, and by 1923 Filipinos comprised more than 90 per cent of the civil service.

But American tutelage had its shortcomings. Despite some noble efforts, the United States never managed to promote a fair deal for peasants; today almost 35 per cent of them are still sharecroppers, and their productivity is one of the lowest in the world. The enormous power of the landlords evolved, in part, from another weakness of U.S. rule in the Philippines. Unlike colonial powers elsewhere in Southeast Asia, which tried first to build efficient administrative structures, the United States gave overwhelming priority to political development. A legislature was established, and political parties were encouraged. Since independence was promised, nationalism was less of an issue than elsewhere in Asia. Without any real ideology to champion, the Philippine politician devoted himself mainly to winning votes, and this frequently made him a pawn of special interest groups, such as landowners or sugar growers. And in performing favors for his supporters, he rendered the services normally provided by the civil service. A wise Filipino in need of a license soon found it expeditious to see his congressman instead of the license bureau, and this sort of custom has led to a good deal of graft and corruption.

Colonialism did not bring the West to all the lands of Southeast Asia. The odd exception was Thailand, which escaped European control through shrewd diplomacy and remained an independent buffer between the British in Burma and the French in Indochina. Though isolated, Thailand's enlightened aristocracy saw the need for modern change and brought western ideas and techniques into the country in a gradual and graceful manner.

MUCH of the initial impulse for this trend came from King Mongkut, a courteous, scholarly man who had spent 26 years as a Buddhist monk before acceding to the throne in 1851. During this monastic period, he reformed the religious code, learned Latin and English from Christian missionaries and, most important, wandered around the countryside familiarizing himself with common people in a way that few royal princes could. His friendship with Europeans led to treaties with Britain and other nations, and western influence entered Thailand for the first time since Dame Golden Horseshoe had popularized custard cakes. A former Belgian politician became Mongkut's general adviser, a Dane headed the provincial police, an Italian major directed the military academy and other Europeans, mostly British, reorganized government departments. Intrigued by other countries' problems as well as his own, Mongkut corresponded with U.S. President James Buchanan, offering him elephants "as improved means of transportation." Due to American climatic conditions, the suggestion was graciously declined. Mongkut also hired an English governess, Anna Leonowens, for his children. Her memoirs eventually evolved into the Hollywood film *The King and I,* a version of court life so fancifully untrue that the picture was banned by the Thais, a people normally prepared to laugh at anything.

Mongkut's heir, King Chulalongkorn, went so much further in introducing modern institutions that his own son later called him a revolutionary. At his coronation in 1873 Chulalongkorn dramatically abolished the custom of prostration in the royal presence. Later he outlawed slavery, created a revenue department and a provincial administration, built railroads, and forced the aristocracy to send their children to the western-type schools he set up in the palace. With all this, the Siamese kings retained a taste for the traditional. Mongkut was an active polygamist, producing 82 children by his 35 wives. Chulalongkorn enjoyed much of the pageantry that attends oriental courts, and he did nothing to discourage such sonorous titles for himself as "Royal Descendant of the Sun Who Shines Like the Finest Jewel" and "Greatest Sovereign of Righteousness."

IMPOSED from above, western influence perhaps had a less profound effect on Thailand's population than it had on other peoples of Southeast Asia. This has given the country more stability than any other in the region. Centuries of independence from foreign control have also left the Thais with little resentment of the West. They approach the European on equal footing, and lack the "colonial complex" often found in other countries of Southeast Asia.

In Thailand as in the rest of Southeast Asia, however, the West's impact launched a whole series of gradual changes. Commercial crops exposed peasants to the vagaries of world markets. The influx of Chinese and Indian traders and bankers created an alien middle class. Cities flourished on the sites of tiny villages, and in these new urban centers there developed the westernized leadership of the future. For the West stirred Asians to find themselves, and even those who later directed struggles for independence recognized their debt to European ideas. Although exiled to the outer islands of eastern Indonesia by the Dutch from 1934 to 1942, the budding nationalist Sutan Sjahrir—later a prime minister of Indonesia—wrote what many young Asians felt at the time: "What we in the East admire most in the West is its indestructible vitality, its love for life and for the fulfillment of life. Every vital young man and young woman in the East ought to look toward the West, for he or she can learn only from the West to regard himself or herself as a center of vitality capable of changing and bettering the world."

THE western impact was also shattering, for it started a process that it could not complete. Unintentionally the West inspired nationalism but did not create nations. It encouraged public health measures without concern for population growth. It introduced schools but prevented the expansion of employment opportunities for those whom it educated. It shook ancient class structures yet did not demolish them, only substituting for an old aristocracy new leaders neither fully modern nor as traditionally stable as their forefathers. And the exposure to western technology, institutions and prestige imbued these new leaders with a sense of speed, with an ambition to achieve in years what formerly took millennia to accomplish. Limited and undigested, western influence has been, above all, disruptive. To judge it in retrospect is perhaps an exercise in futility. It was, as the Swiss scholar Herbert Luethy has remarked, "neither a chain of crimes nor a chain of beneficence: it was the birth of the modern world itself."

The country club of Saigon, built when Vietnam was French, is a reminder of the elegant life once enjoyed by European colonists.

Varied Faces of a World in Transition

Five hundred years of European trade and conquest had an immense impact on Southeast Asia. The people developed a taste for western comforts, western-style government and independence. Yet they did not acquire the complex political and industrial machinery that make a modern state viable. For every mine or factory there are many thousands of farmers scratching the soil with primitive tools, and democracy struggles against ancient privilege and poverty.

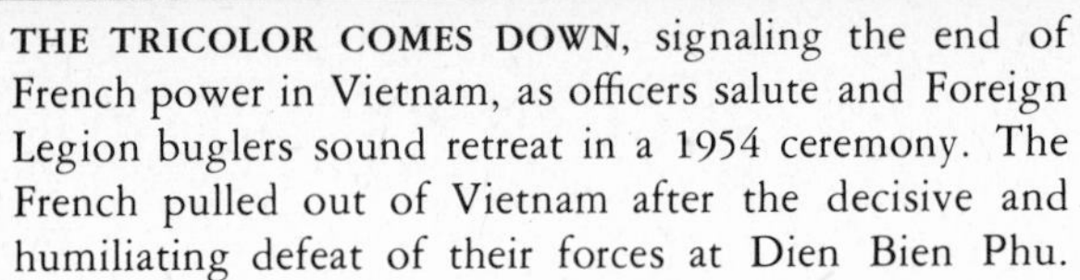

THE TRICOLOR COMES DOWN, signaling the end of French power in Vietnam, as officers salute and Foreign Legion buglers sound retreat in a 1954 ceremony. The French pulled out of Vietnam after the decisive and humiliating defeat of their forces at Dien Bien Phu.

DUTCH FAMILIES LEAVE, sailing home from Djakarta. Following Indonesian independence in 1949, some 46,000 colonials chose to stay. But anti-imperialist feeling steadily grew and in 1957 all remaining Dutch were ordered out of the country and their property was seized.

THE OLD ORDER PASSES as colonials strike their flags and sail for home

DEMOCRACY has taken firm root in the Philippines, but the islands' political vigor has not been matched by social or economic progress

SLUM DWELLERS who live without plumbing draw water at a public faucet *(left)*, while behind them a government housing project extends the promise of a better life.

DISMAL POVERTY forces a Filipino family to find shelter among ruined walls in an old quarter of Manila *(right)*. This area is being razed for housing projects, but many urban Filipinos still live in slums, and farmers are little better off. Some 20 per cent of the work force suffers from chronic unemployment or underemployment.

ELECTION POSTERS *(below)* line a busy road outside Manila during a bitterly fought 1965 presidential race in which Ferdinand Marcos unseated Diosdado Macapagal.

IN ROYAL REGALIA, King Bhumibol and Queen Sirikit pose for a formal portrait in front of a nine-tiered parasol, traditional symbol of Thailand's Chakri Dynasty.

OBSERVING A YEARLY RITUAL at dawn on New Year's Day, Thailand's royal couple present food to Buddhist monks, a rite that confers spiritual merit on the donors.

THAILAND, untouched by colonialism, displays a pleasing blend of east and west

INDONESIAN WOMEN, awarded full political rights in 1955, line up in festive dress to vote for the first time. In spite of such outward shows of democracy, Indonesia's government has become increasingly totalitarian.

Nationalism's Seductive Fervor

WEARING a traditional costume, Prince Norodom Sihanouk faces thousands of Cambodians jammed into a Phnompenh stadium, and there is magnetic exultation in his measured tones. He laughs and whispers, cries, shouts and sighs as he evokes the past grandeur of the great Khmer Empire. He warns against present enemies, and promises the fulfillment of some future destiny. The crescendo of his oratory cues the national anthem, and the crowd drifts away, bemused and exalted, somehow feeling Cambodian.

At its most intense, such is the seductive fervor of nationalism in Southeast Asia, and to different degrees it is felt everywhere. Nationalism is evident in Saigon editorials that warn darkly of "neo-imperialism" and in the popular Philippine campaign theme of "Filipinos First." It inspires Javanese to point proudly to ancient Majapahit power, and it moves North Borneo mountaineers to claim a common tribal affiliation. Often anachronistic, sometimes fanatic and rarely rational, nationalism is the strongest sentiment in these newly sovereign lands which grope for constructive political beliefs and institutions.

Many Southeast Asians fought western nations to achieve their independence, but their nationalism was catalyzed and cultivated by western rule. It grew, in part, from the positive European endowments of education and culture, with their emphasis on individual dignity and humanism. Nationalism also evolved from the negative anger and frustrations these very benefits engendered among a literate, politically aware minority. Vietnamese schooled by the French learned that *liberté, égalité* and *fraternité* were principles, not practices to be observed; qualified Indonesians were oddly unacceptable for higher government jobs in the Dutch administration, and Burmese and Indians were social pariahs.

BUT above such acute tensions, there was another, overwhelmingly pervasive force at work—the disintegration of European order. European nations had inadvertently brought to Southeast Asia—as to other parts of the world—more stability than the area had ever known. But while these powers were carrying peace and security to the corners of the earth, they were destroying themselves at home. To Asians, World War I was a "European civil war" that demolished the moral foundations of Europe's prestige. Atop this catastrophe came the great depression of the 1930s, which devastated colonial economies, and this disaster was followed by a final European humiliation: defeat by the Japanese. By the end of World War II, Europe's authority was in shambles, and it fell to inexperienced, unprepared groups of native nationalists to build something viable out of the ruins.

Nationalism had grown gradually in Southeast Asia, and logically enough, it germinated earliest in the most westernized country of the area. For more than three centuries, Spanish control of the Philippines had been relatively relaxed. But in the mid-19th Century, Manila was opened to world trade, and soon a small middle class burgeoned. About the same time, however, a harsh, ruthless breed of Spanish official flocked to the Philippines from Spain's lost territories in America. A few educated Filipinos and Philippine-born Spaniards protested against these corrupt carpetbaggers. Among them was a prodigious young physician and writer, José Rizal. He was destined to personify the cause of Philippine nationalism.

Rizal wrote poems and novels attacking Spain's repressive regime in the Philippines. Although he advocated only mild legal reforms, he was charged with "rebellion, sedition and illicit association." On a December morning in 1896 he was executed by a firing squad. Overnight Rizal became a martyr, and his death touched off a wave of violence. A clever youth named Emilio Aguinaldo assumed leadership of a new revolutionary movement that battled against the Spanish for two years. When American troops invaded the Philippines in 1898 during the Spanish-American War, Aguinaldo's forces joined them and together they defeated the Spanish. At this juncture, however, they parted ways. The Filipinos had been fighting for independence; the United States, as far as anyone could reckon, had been fighting for the Philippines. Scarcely had the shooting stopped than a new war broke out between Filipinos and Americans—the only real colonial conflict in U.S. history. Before it ended in 1902, more than 4,000 Americans, some 20,000 Filipino soldiers and guerrillas and more than 200,000 civilians had died.

ANTI-IMPERIALISTS in the United States angrily denounced the conquest of the Philippines. Senator George Frisbie Hoar of Massachusetts predicted that the Filipinos would become "sullen and irreconcilable enemies, possessed of a hatred which centuries cannot eradicate." This prophecy, of course, proved ludicrous. As it turned out, United States tutelage was benevolent, and no people today are more deeply pro-American than the Filipinos. Indeed, they feel so intimate with the United States that many Philippine politicians seem to exert themselves in affirming their nationalism, as if to remind the world that their country is sovereign.

Throughout Southeast Asia—as in many other underdeveloped areas—the peculiarities and particularities of nationalism similarly reflect colonial experiences. In contrast to the Americans in the Philippines, the Dutch in Indonesia did little to encourage political maturity, and Indonesian nationalism consequently evolved as an angry antidote to colonialism.

ISLAM has none of the fervor in Indonesia that it displays in the Middle East, yet it provided the first framework for nationalist solidarity. In 1911, when the Sarekat Islam (Islamic Association) was formed, it was primarily a union of Moslem merchants anxious to protect themselves against their Chinese competitors. The Dutch tried to restrict its activities, but before long it had acquired 800,000 members and a distinctly secular, political flavor. Soon other movements mushroomed, some thriving, some dying quickly. Inspired by the Russian Revolution, a Dutch engineer named Hendrik Sneevliet—later an important Soviet agent in Asia—founded what in 1920 became the Indonesian Communist Party. With confused instructions from Moscow, the Communists blindly attempted to stage their revolution by a series of terrorist actions, and they were easy prey for the Dutch. By 1927 a new nationalist group had made its appearance—the Perserikatan Nasional Indonesia, led by a dynamic new leader, Sukarno.

As an engineering student at Bandung, Sukarno had been instrumental in creating "study groups" which eventually became the National Party of Indonesia. The *Bung,* or brother, as Sukarno likes to be called, was not a serious intellectual. But he was graceful and charming, and he perfected the art of persuasion, a political asset in the Orient far more important than plans or programs. By the time he reached 26, Sukarno had become the liveliest nationalist in the country. He reinterpreted Indonesian history to inflate past glory; he promised a glowing future; and he recounted tales of Dutch "greed and ferocity." Sukarno had reached such stature by 1929 that he was arrested by the Dutch and convicted of "subversion." Except for a 20-month period of freedom, he spent the next 13 years in jail or exiled to the remote islands of the archipelago.

Sukarno did not invent Indonesian nationalism; rather, he skillfully represented, channelized and guided a sentiment that was spreading among his educated compatriots. Rejected by the Dutch, Indonesian intellectuals began to speak Bahasa Indonesia, a modernized form of Malay, and to wear the *pitji,* a black fez, to symbolize their national identity. These were indications of a growing frustration on their part, but the Dutch seemed oblivious to the unrest in the islands. They severely repressed even the mildest nationalists and disregarded appeals for the most innocuous reforms. In one instance they rejected an Indonesian suggestion for representation, couching their response in a classic specimen of Blimpish prose: "The system of government now in progress will create, in due time, a basis for autonomy on the lower levels of administration, out of which may arise the possibility of forming autonomous institutions on a somewhat higher level which, ultimately, will lead to the granting of a larger share of autonomy."

IN defense of their failure to prepare Indonesia for self-government, the Dutch argued with reason—as they still do—that the archipelago, with its scattering of diverse peoples, had no genuine national identity. But in Indochina, where the native nationalist sentiment was also ignored, similar claims by the French were far less valid. The Vietnamese had been a nation for centuries, and they never fully acquiesced to French domination. Every decade was punctuated by some rebellion, mutiny or strike, and the French themselves confusingly contributed to the unrest. True to their belief in their civilizing mission, they diffused the works of such precursors of the French Revolution as Rousseau and Montesquieu but arrested young intellectuals who repeated the themes of that upheaval. They forcibly recruited 100,000 Vietnamese for service in France during World War I, overlooking the obvious danger that these men would return from the West with modern ideas and a desire for change in their homeland.

A vast variety of nationalist movements and individuals sprouted in Vietnam between the wars, and out of all this ferment came a single, strong individual who was an equally fervent Communist. His real name is still unknown, but the most famous of his many aliases is Ho Chi Minh—"He who enlightens."

The son of a minor government official dismissed for political activities, Ho was 19 when he went abroad as a cabin boy. He sailed throughout the world and landed finally in London, where he became a dishwasher at the Carlton Hotel, and during World War I he went to Paris. There he found work as a photographer's assistant and led a solitary, industrious existence. Ho's only outlet was politics, and in the freedom of the French capital he was able to behave as he could never have in Vietnam. He attended the meetings of a local debating society and joined the French Socialist party, and when the Paris Peace Conference convened in 1919, he sent the leaders of the victorious allied powers a memorandum calling for the application of President Woodrow Wilson's principles of self-determination of peoples to Vietnam. The document was, of course, disregarded.

Within a year Ho was a member of the newly organized French Communist party, and as a cog in the Communist apparatus he traveled extensively in Europe and Asia. During this time he laid the foundations of his "League for the Independence of Vietnam," known colloquially as the Viet Minh when it rose to action after World War II.

A CONFUSION OVER NAMES

To Westerners, a minor mystery (and a major annoyance) in Southeast Asia is the bewildering confusion of personal names–and with reason. Until western or western-style administrators began urging their adoption, most Southeast Asians had no family names.

When family names were taken, the practices varied. In Cambodia, family names precede given names; thus the family name of a man known as Pich Sabay would be Pich. He would generally be addressed by both. In Laos and Thailand the family name of one Bounma Santivong would be Santivong, but he would be addressed as Bounma. In Vietnam, however, Nguyen Van Hung, whose family name is Nguyen, would be called Hung.

Many Southeast Asians, like Indonesia's president, Sukarno, still use only one name. Burmese also use only a single name. Their names are usually prefixed by a title like U, which indicates that the man addressed is a person of some stature.

It may be understandable that nationalism in Indonesia and Indochina, forged in the furnace of oppressive rule, should have been extremist. But it is perhaps less clear why Burmese today recall the time under British control as a period of severe subjugation. Over the years, the British conceded a visible measure of self-government to the Burmese, and by the outbreak of World War II, the colony had a constitution, a legislature and a prime minister of its own. To the Burmese, however, most of these concessions seemed illusory.

The earliest forerunners of nationalism in Burma were calm, courteous, English-trained barristers who proclaimed that "we speak English and appreciate the western way of life . . . we are gentlemen." As early as the mid-1930s, however, a noisier and younger generation had come along. They were upset by the depression, which had devastated the Burmese rice economy, and they jealously feared that the British would grant greater autonomy to India than to Burma. Strangely enough, these cantankerous youths operated out of the British-run University of Rangoon.

The most active of these callow nationalists were a morose young man named Aung San, who studied English literature, political science and European history, and a more mature law student called Nu, who later became Prime Minister U Nu. They challenged the university officials, indiscriminately libeled British authorities and rival groups in the student newspaper, and used the student union as a strike instrument. After leaving the university, they joined a small, vocal group of extreme nationalists known as the Thakins—ironically, a respectful term, like sahib in India—and attempted to sabotage British preparations for World War II.

Aung San was the more dynamic of the two young nationalists. Inspired by totalitarian concepts of force and uniformity, he created a private army in 1939. The Japanese considered these irregulars a potential fifth column for their impending conquest of Burma and offered to train 30 of Aung San's officers. He accepted. The "Thirty Comrades"—now part of modern Burmese mythology—pooled their blood in a silver bowl, drank to independence and under Japanese auspices formed the Burma Independence Army to fight the British. Aung San took the title of *Bo Teza* (Fire General); another officer, Shu Maung, called himself *Ne Win* (Sun of Glory)—and he still uses this *nom de guerre*. Eventually Aung San switched to the Allied side in the war, and had he not been assassinated by a political rival in 1947 he would probably be prime minister of Burma now.

Aung San was not the only Southeast Asian to enlist Japanese support. Ever since 1905, when it defeated the Russians at Port Arthur, Japan had been admired in the Orient as an Asian nation which had effectively used western techniques against a European power. By 1938, however, when their "Greater East Asia Co-Prosperity Sphere" was proclaimed, the Japanese were projecting a less brilliant image. Japanese aggression had laid waste to China, and it was uncertain whether their occupation of Southeast Asia would mean liberation from colonialism or a worse kind of imperialism.

THEN came the attack on Pearl Harbor, and Japan swept southward. Within six months it controlled every bit of Southeast Asia, from Burma across the Indonesian archipelago and up through the Philippines. Asian troops in canvas shoes had tumbled the great British bases of Hong Kong and Singapore, defeated the United States in the Philippines, driven the Dutch from Java and enveloped the decadent Vichy French regime in Indochina. Thailand, which had no choice but to become Japan's "ally," was turned into an occupied country, used by the Japanese as a source of rice and a strategic route to the south.

Publicly the Japanese announced a policy of "Asia for the Asians," but privately they envisaged a network of satellite areas designed "to advance the national fortunes of the Empire." Southeast Asians were unaware of this secret program, and they reacted to the Japanese in diverse ways. Some resisted from the start. Guerrilla units were formed in Malaya, Vietnam and the Philippines—forces which were to a large extent led by Communists whose aim was not only to overthrow the Japanese but to establish Communist states in those countries. In contrast, many common people were initially impressed by the way the Japanese forced their former white masters to perform the humiliating labor that Asians were made to do before.

THEY soon discovered, however, that the Japanese could be as brutal toward Orientals as they were to Europeans. Natives were commandeered into work gangs, jailed, beaten, tortured and spied upon. Japanese troops were even cruel in their everyday conduct. In Burma, for example, people welcomed the "liberators" and brought them food. "We expected the Japanese commander to be very thankful for our bowls of rice," recounted a peasant, "but all he did was to take his hand out of his trousers pocket and give us a hard slap in the face."

Despite their arrogant and selfish conduct, the Japanese brought significant changes to the area. Their creation of labor, propaganda and other organizations unintentionally engendered a new collectivist spirit. Japanese-backed youth associations detached young people from their elders, inevitably weakening the bonds of tradition. Japan armed and trained natives, and in Indonesia the imperial army sponsored a local force of 120,000 men which later served the nationalists handily. And without enhancing their own reputation, the Japanese finally effaced the last vestiges of western prestige. It was a revolutionary day in Djakarta when the *beo*, a talking bird at the zoo, ceased to speak Dutch and started amusing children in Indonesian.

In India, Jawaharlal Nehru had warned his followers that reliance on the Japanese against the colonial powers was "a remedy worse than the disease," and many Southeast Asian nationalists found this assessment correct. The Burmese were disillusioned to discover that their "autonomous" administration had to follow Japanese military dictates lest its members have their fingernails "manicured," or pulled out, by the Kempeitai, Japan's Gestapo. Even after Burma was declared independent in August 1943, the Japanese army ruled harshly. Their railway into Thailand reportedly cost the lives of 30,000 Burmese workers.

THERE were fewer deceptions in the Philippines, where a Japanese-guided "independent republic" was set up under ex-Supreme Court Justice José Laurel, who collaborated "to mitigate the sufferings of our people and ensure the survival of the Filipino race." In Indonesia, some nationalists went underground, but Sukarno sincerely believed the war was the "golden opportunity" for freedom, and he collaborated with the Japanese. But they stalled on promises of freedom time and again, and it was not until August 17, 1945—eight days after the second atomic bomb fell on Nagasaki—that Sukarno was finally able to proclaim the independence of Indonesia.

European authority in Southeast Asia was gone when World War II ended, and Britain's Labour government recognized this fact. It gracefully agreed to freedom for Burma and, after proper astrological calculation, the actual transfer of power took place at 4:20 a.m. on January 4, 1948. The United States had long promised independence to the Philippines, and it was granted in 1946. In other regions, however, European powers refused to withdraw, and the postwar period was bloody and bitter. There was savage fighting in Java, where armed Indonesians ran amuck (to use a word of Malay origin) against the Dutch while the British tried to keep order. Finally, in December 1949, after four years of warfare and abortive negotiations, the Netherlands agreed to recognize an independent Indonesian republic.

Even more brutal was the struggle for Indochina. For one brief moment in March 1946, Ho Chi Minh and the French Commissioner in Hanoi had agreed to a Democratic Republic of Vietnam which would maintain ties with France. But extremists in both the French and Vietnamese camps sabotaged the compromise. Actual war broke out in 1946, and for almost eight years the cream of France's professional soldiers vainly tried to defeat the elusive Viet Minh guerrillas. The French enticed the corpulent playboy emperor Bao Dai to establish a rival Vietnamese government, but he was no match for ascetic Ho Chi Minh, who succeeded in mustering popular support that bordered on hero worship.

France was finally defeated in 1954 at Dien Bien Phu, and the painful years of war had a far-reaching effect on Vietnam. The Communists had successfully captured leadership of the nationalist movement, converting some of its members and eliminating others. When the 1954 Geneva Conference divided Vietnam, President Ngo Dinh Diem's government in the south suffered badly from a lack of competent, educated Vietnamese, and his administration was not a success.

Within slightly more than a decade after the end of World War II, almost every land in Southeast Asia was independent. Even anomalous Singapore, a city populated largely by ethnic Chinese, had become an autonomous state of the British Commonwealth, and there was pressure for freedom on the part of budding nationalist movements in the outlying British colonies of Sarawak and North Borneo.

MORE of a crusade than an ideology, nationalism was focused on a single, uncomplicated goal—independence. Its dynamism was in men and action rather than ideas and institutions. Most of the nationalists who won sovereignty for their countries went on to become the leaders of Southeast Asia's states, and their present governments are more a mirror of their personalities than of any particular political ideologies.

As always in this fragmented region, there are exceptions to that generalization. There is a precise structure of government in the Philippines. Patterned on the U.S. model, it balances executive, judicial and legislative branches; and as in the United States, the president is under pressure from Congress, his own party and a wide variety of vested interests. Democracy in the Philippines may be racy and flamboyant, but it functions, and the country's political maturity is unmatched anywhere else in Southeast Asia.

IN stark contrast, Laos has only begun to shake off its medieval traces and it is, as someone has said, "hurtling headlong into the 15th Century." There are no real politics in Laos. Instead, an assortment of feudal princes skirmishes for power, and since Laos has been thrown into the international arena, they have dutifully attached modern labels to their movements, calling themselves "neutralists" or "anti-Communists." They are mainly motivated by ancient rivalries and family ties, and only Prince Souphanouvong, nominal head of the pro-Communist Pathet Lao, has been exposed to contemporary ideas in his Marxist indoctrination.

In the nearly two decades after Indonesia attained independence, its government largely reflected the character of Sukarno, who managed the country single-handedly. Born under the sign of Gemini, Sukarno claimed that he could "mix with Communists, Socialists, Moslems, Christians, revolutionary nationalists and even compromising nationalists." Over the years, however, he allied himself increasingly with Indonesia's Communists, until his leanings to the Left upset his balance.

His downfall came after an abortive Communist coup d'état in late 1965 opened the way for a military takeover. Headed by General Suharto, the new army regime gradually corroded Sukarno's authority, then dramatically reversed his policies. It banned the Indonesian Communist Party following a period in which hundreds of thousands of real and suspected Communists were massacred. It also unraveled Indonesia's formerly close ties with Red China. And among other moves, the army and its civilian advisers abandoned the concept of "revolutionary romanticism" promoted by Sukarno, replacing it with more sensible, pragmatic economic strategies. The flamboyant, poetic pronouncements that characterized Sukarno's years in office gave way to prose.

Yet the new regime inherited a country that was literally bankrupt. Its foreign debt of over $2.5 billion, for example, demanded interest payments and other servicing that took more than Indonesia's annual earnings from its exports. Its internal economy had deteriorated to such abysmal depths that, Indonesians quip, "anyone who is not totally confused is just very badly informed." Still, through the sheer force of his personality, Sukarno had more or less held the sprawling archipelago republic together, giving its mosaic of ethnic groups a certain sense of national identity that is not likely to splinter in the foreseeable future.

IN endowing his country with a measure of cohesion, Sukarno succeeded where Burma's former Prime Minister U Nu failed. Pious and gentle, U Nu tailored his political behavior to the Buddhist principles of trust and tolerance. He adopted neutralism because it meant "peace and friendship with all countries." But U Nu's charming good will was not enough to defeat rebel minorities or tame unruly politicians. Early in 1962, General Ne Win staged a coup d'état and established a military government. Stern and serious, he has isolated the country from the outside world, curbing political freedom to restore orderly administration. It still remains to be seen, however, whether Burma can begin to make genuine progress.

Government in Cambodia is entirely in the hands of Prince Norodom Sihanouk, an energetic, often perplexing man in his early forties. Sihanouk has jailed his country's Communists, yet has sent three of his 30 children—by an indeterminate number of wives and concubines—to school in Peking, where they have been given

Marxist training. He refuses to join either of the world's power blocs and considers himself strictly neutral, but he believes that Red China will eventually take over all of Southeast Asia.

If his foreign policy is frequently bewildering, Sihanouk is a hero to his own people. He forced the French to grant independence to Cambodia in 1953, a year before the Geneva Conference, and he skillfully persuaded the Communist Viet Minh to evacuate his territory. Since then he has used foreign aid—contributed from almost everywhere—to generate a modest economic program. He likes to go out into the countryside himself to help in road building, sometimes inviting the diplomatic corps to join in, and refreshing them afterwards with a champagne luncheon. At elections Sihanouk invariably wins 99 per cent of the votes.

In large measure, the shortcomings of South Vietnam's embattled regime stem from the late President Ngo Dinh Diem's nine years in office. While courageous and honest, Diem was a traditionalist whose autocratic rule failed to generate the widespread popular support it needed to defend itself against a determined Communist insurgency deeply rooted in the countryside. Moreover, the rigid, repressive measures promoted by Diem's family, particularly against South Vietnam's Buddhists, provoked an uprising that resulted in the overthrow of the Saigon government late in 1963. The deterioration of South Vietnam's political establishment in the years after that was a factor in prompting the United States to begin its bombing of Communist North Vietnam as well as to intervene with American troops in the widening Vietnam war. To many specialists familiar with the Vietnam situation, however, the country's capacity to meet the Communist challenge will depend on its ability to develop an effective government.

THAILAND'S late prime minister, Marshal Sarit Thanarat, who died in 1963, was an exceptionally corrupt dictator. But paradoxically, his rather old-fashioned oriental despotism was benevolent. As a consequence, Thailand achieved a measure of stability and prosperity during Sarit's six years of rule. Many Thais, therefore, tend to look back on the late prime minister's peculations as "a premium we paid for progress."

Marshal Thanom Kittikachorn, who has been the Thai prime minister since Marshal Sarit's death, is an amiable, relatively easy-going army officer. His regime has been less a one-man show than a military oligarchy directed by several generals. While more or less benign, this "group dictatorship" has notably failed to deal effectively with Thailand's underdeveloped Northeast, where a Communist insurgency appears to have been gaining ground. At the same time, however, Thailand has abandoned its traditional middle-of-the-road international position by permitting the United States to use its air bases to bomb North Vietnam.

MALAYSIA has a British-type Parliament, but perhaps nowhere in Southeast Asia has a politician's personality proved so important. Prime Minister Abdul Rahman—also called *Tunku,* or prince, has managed to balance the divergent Malay and Chinese communities through the strength of his own persuasive moderation. The seventh child of a native sultan, the *Tunku* was a playboy in his youth. He was almost expelled from Cambridge and did not pass his bar exams until he was past 40. But he sobered up during the cruel Japanese occupation of Malaya, and after getting into politics by accident, he led the country to independence within the British Commonwealth in 1957. He has used Malaya's rubber and tin profits wisely, and he discards grandiose schemes in favor of pragmatic attitudes. "We must be practical," he says. "We want peace, harmony and good business, and the hell with hifalutin' political ideas."

Reaching out from his narrow peninsula, Abdul Rahman federated Malaya with Singapore and the former British-controlled areas of Sarawak and North Borneo to create the new state of Malaysia. The predominantly Chinese island of Singapore has since left the federation, once again altering Southeast Asia's changing map.

British-trained police swing down a street in Kuala Lumpur in 1957, celebrating the independence of the Federation of Malaya.

Perils and Problems of the Newly Free

When independence came to Southeast Asia few of the new nations were ready to meet its challenges. Most were burdened with high levels of illiteracy, low levels of political experience and economies that resisted change. Independence did not bring the promised ease and affluence. Frustrated leaders have lost patience with democracy, dictatorial regimes have sprung up, and the specter of civil strife, as in Vietnam, threatens progress everywhere.

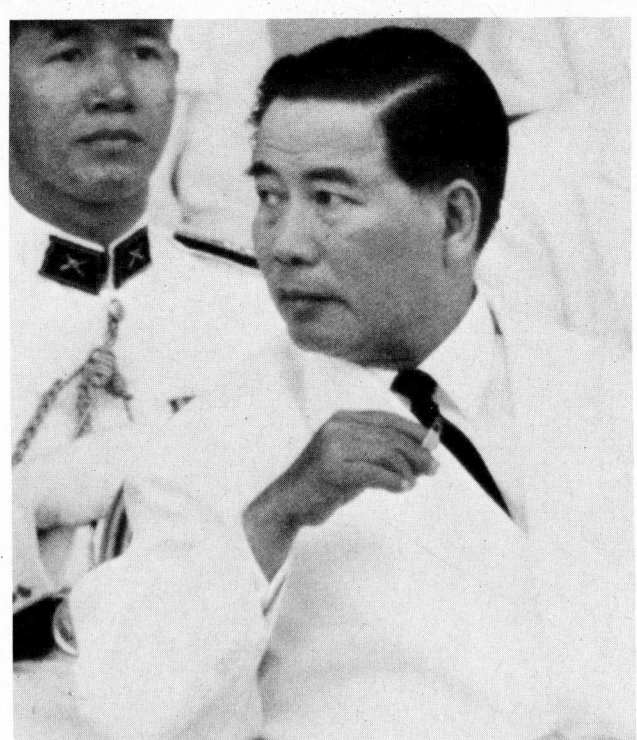

MURDERED PRESIDENT, Ngo Dinh Diem ruled South Vietnam for nearly a decade following independence from France. In 1963, his unpopular and autocratic regime was toppled, and he and his brother were killed.

STERN NATIONALIST, Ho Chi Minh *(left)* governs Communist North Vietnam. Following World War II, he waged a crafty war to expel the French, and since then has dedicated his energy to the reunification of Vietnam.

IN DIVIDED VIETNAM, the North's Ho Chi Minh has outlasted a series of South Vietnamese leaders

ABLE GENERAL, Nguyen Van Thieu *(above)* emerged as the winner following the intense political maneuvering that preceded South Vietnam's first freely held presidential election carried out in September 1967.

DASHING AIRMAN, Nguyen Cao Ky *(above)* advanced swiftly to become chief of South Vietnam's air force and, in 1965, to lead the country as head of a military junta. The junta, despite talk of democracy, ruled by decree.

MILITARY TRIUMVIRATE, Duon Van Minh, Tran Thien Khiem and Nguyen Khanh together led one of the bewildering succession of ineffectual governments in Saigon that followed the overthrow of the Diem regime.

INDONESIA, after two decades of revolution and anti-imperialist fever under Sukarno, finally awakened to find itself a bankrupt nation

STRIPPED OF POWER, an aging President Sukarno *(above)* reads a statement to the press in the summer of 1966, while his nemesis and eventual successor, General Suharto, looks on. The left-leaning Sukarno, not content with having welded a nation out of the diverse peoples of the former Dutch East Indies, proceeded to wreck his country's economy by neglect and wasteful spending.

THE ABANDONED SKELETON of a half-finished trade center in Djakarta, one of many aborted projects begun by Sukarno, stands as a monument to his reckless fiscal policies.

A RED CHINESE STUDENT is attacked in Djakarta in 1965, following anti-Communist riots that took some 350,000 lives and annihilated the Communist Party in Indonesia.

REFORMER, Philippine President Ferdinand Marcos *(above)* leads in the struggle to eradicate widespread crime and corruption from his government.

EX-KING, Prince Norodom Sihanouk of Cambodia *(right)*, who left his throne to become Prime Minister, steers a neutral course between East and West.

ABLE EXECUTIVE, Marshal Thanom Kittikachorn, who has been Thailand's Prime Minister since 1963, has worked toward closer ties with the United States.

TOUGH ASCETIC, General Ne Win of Burma heads a socialist bureaucracy that has nationalized more than 90 per cent of the troubled nation's industry.

LEADERS, all veterans of the struggle for independence, share the task of guiding their nations into the modern world

NEUTRALIST, Laos's Premier Prince Souvanna Phouma heads a "troika" government, representing pro-Communist, neutralist and Right-Wing elements.

DEMOCRAT, Malaysia's Prime Minister Tunku Abdul Rahman heads Southeast Asia's most prosperous nation, forged from former British colonies.

MASSED RANKS of bicycles, scooters and motor bikes completely fill a parking lot in Saigon while their owners watch a soccer game. Vietnamese workers long to own bikes and, despite low wages, many of them do.

5

Expectations, Illusions and Inertia

MOST of Southeast Asia's states have been independent for only a short time. In this period they have tried to break away from centuries of tradition and adjust to the modern world. Freedom has been exhilarating, but hasty attempts at change, compressed into so short a span, have been sometimes chaotic, largely uneven. Village life has hardly altered. By contrast, the region's crowded, sprawling cities are precocious, effervescent, volatile—and simmering with problems.

The cities of Southeast Asia are recent inventions. Singapore has grown from a swampy island to a lively metropolis in less than 150 years. Small cities at the turn of the century, Saigon, Bangkok and Manila now have populations of more than a million. Barely 100 years ago Kuala Lumpur was founded at the jungle confluence of two rivers and suitably given the name that means "muddy juncture"; now it is a bustling city of 400,000, with shiny skyscrapers and traffic-clogged streets.

There is a vital pace of change in these cities, and nothing better portrays their air of new freedom than the sight of urban women. Many are emancipated and busy, and they have adopted the styles of western femininity. They use cosmetics and wear daring mini-skirts, and they can be seen playing tennis in frilly shorts. They drive cars and work in offices, and some run for parliament or agitate in trade unions. What mainly distinguishes them from their country cousins—and from their mothers as well—is their opposition to prearranged marriage and, among many, their intense desire for education.

The same serious drive for knowledge and training is shared by all of Southeast Asia's youth, and they gravitate to the cities to go to colleges and universities. Unlike their more idealistic fathers, they are mostly practical-minded. They want the status of a diploma and the chance for a good job later, and they study science, engineering, business and medicine. Most students today still come from well-to-do families, which not only can afford educational costs but do not have to depend on a son's or a daughter's earnings for additional income. But even poor boys somehow struggle for degrees.

Ko San Myint majors in mathematics and physics at the University of Rangoon. He started out with a total capital of 180 *kyats* ($38), one fourth of his father's life savings. To help meet expenses he found a tutoring job for 100 *kyats* ($21) per month, and he shares a single room with two other equally impecunious comrades, the three of them sleeping on the floor and reading under the same naked light bulb. When they graduate, however, Ko San Myint and his friends will face an even more difficult problem. Jobs are scarce in Burma, where three out of every four university graduates still look for "decent employment" a year after graduation.

ALL the states of Southeast Asia have made great strides in expanding their educational facilities, from grade school through university levels, and thousands of college graduates pour forth every year. But democratization has meant a sharp drop in standards from preindependence days. More important, the region's economies have not grown in proportion to the increasing number of university-educated youth. In places like Burma, Indonesia and Singapore, some disoriented graduates have succumbed to the blandishments of Marxist agitators, who claim that there are more dynamic opportunities in Communist societies. But most young people tend to be easygoing and apathetic, and several professors and officials wish the younger generation were more rebellious. "The Filipino youth has grown indifferent," says former Philippine Secretary of Education Alejandro R. Roces. "His idealism and irascibility have been watered down. It will take a rallying point . . . to jolt him from his complacency. And only his elders can provide this."

NOR are urban youths the only disenchanted ones. Peasants pour into cities like Bangkok and Rangoon at the rate of 200 or more per day, hoping for factory work. But nowhere have industries developed quickly enough to absorb these numbers, and many cities have become large, unwieldy receptacles for a dislocated, restless, unemployed or underemployed proletariat. Almost one fourth of Djakarta's population of 3.5 million are squatters, working only occasionally and eating frugally. Uprooted from their villages, they dare not return to the countryside, and they are disillusioned.

Interviewed by the American writer Willard Hanna not long ago, a Djakarta *betjak* (pedicab) driver explained—probably with some exaggeration—that he ate rice only once in two days, that he occasionally had fish but never meat and that his family's clothes were rags. "Now we are free," he said, "and the big plantations belong to us, and the Dutch have left behind their fine houses and their fine cars and it all belongs to us. But I haven't a fine house. And I don't have a fine car or even a bicycle. I haven't even a *betjak* of my own. . . ."

In most of Southeast Asia's countries, the realities of independence have not measured up to hopes. In part, expectations were inflated by nationalists anxious to win popular support. And many of the region's leaders, idealistically believing their own propaganda, were sincerely convinced that they would automatically inherit European commercial enterprises, which all seemed so prosperous. Thus they concentrated on politics and their own prestige, and paid scant attention to the complexities of economic development.

After Burma achieved independence, for example, Prime Minister U Nu and his colleagues proceeded to fulfill their dream of creating a socialist state. They nationalized foreign timber concessions and the British-owned inland water transport company, and they established a government monopoly to control the sale of rice, the country's main export. They built a pharmaceutical plant to manufacture vitamin pills (which few people wanted), and they constructed a steel mill to process wartime scrap metal (which soon ran out). Only years later did U Nu seem to grasp what had gone wrong. With characteristic candor, he confessed: "We lack managerial skills, and without them, nationalization can be a mess."

The blunders of mismanagement have been even more dramatic in Indonesia, a region of remarkable natural wealth. Potentially, Indonesia can supply 40 per cent of the world's rubber and 20 per cent of its tin, and it is said to contain the world's fourth largest oil reserves. It is rich in copra, palm oil, tobacco and coffee, and it has untapped veins of iron ore and bauxite. Some of its soil is so fertile that, as an American economist has put it, "you can shove a stick into the ground and it will sprout leaves." But with all these gifts, the country's economy has gradually disintegrated. Except for oil—extracted by foreign companies—production of Indonesia's principal export commodities has declined steadily during recent years. At the same time, inflation has rendered the currency worthless, and the government is chronically crippled by a shortage of funds.

MUCH of this trouble stems from years of mismanagement under former President Sukarno. In 1959, for example, Sukarno whimsically cut the value of banknotes and froze bank deposits without even alerting his own finance officials. This move was aimed at reducing inflation, but it so shattered confidence in the country's currency that everyone unloaded his *rupiahs,* and within a year banknote circulation had increased 92 per cent. Sukarno's campaigns to take West New Guinea from the Dutch and "crush" neighboring Malaysia led to staggering military expenditures, including a debt of more than one billion dollars to the Soviet Union for weapons. Since 1967, Sukarno's successors led by General Suharto have tried to bring order into Indonesia's chaotic economy by scuttling old controls and bringing free market forces to bear. However, their persecution of some three million overseas Chinese has grievously disrupted the internal commercial network. Most experts concur that Suharto's government has a difficult task ahead.

SEVERAL countries of Southeast Asia have wisely used foreign assistance for such constructive projects as roads, power plants, airports, schools, hospitals and experimental agriculture stations. Under international auspices, a huge operation is beginning that will develop the winding Mekong River. United States military aid has been essential for the defenses of Vietnam, Thailand, Cambodia and other states. But however generous it is, foreign assistance is no guarantee of economic growth, and the region's two major recipients of American help—South Vietnam and Laos—have not made any notable long-term economic progress.

Laos, which has received the highest per capita amount of American assistance in the world, has in fact been the scene of a shockingly futile aid program. In 1955, when Southeast Asia seemed to be in critical straits following the Indochina war, U.S. Secretary of State John Foster Dulles decreed that Laos be made an "anti-Communist bastion." The little country, whose only cash crop is opium, was so primitive that economists warned that an influx of capital would disrupt its elementary economy. For political reasons, however, some $40 million per year was funneled into Laos. In principle, the dollars were to be doled out to local businessmen to subsidize their imports, which would be sold to produce the income necessary to maintain the army. In reality, the whole program turned into a frenzy of private profiteering that, as an American aid official later wrote, had "an almost fairy tale implausibility."

Instead of importing merchandise, traders connived with Laotian politicians to obtain dollars, which they used for black market currency manipulations. Or import licenses were issued for goods that never reached Laos, being sold instead for a higher return in Bangkok and other cities. Incalculable sums of money were made in shady operations of one sort or another. The once-sleepy capital of Vientiane became crowded with new Mercedes cars—a status symbol of wealth in Asia—and affluent government officials built themselves hideously luxurious houses. Periodic attempts have been made to eradicate corruption in Laos, but most of the efforts have been fruitless.

Corruption is traditional in the Orient. For centuries the Chinese have played a game—somewhat like Monopoly—called "Advancement in Officialdom," in which players move higher in a fictitious bureaucracy and thereby collect money from those in lower ranks. But the custom is more than a sport in all the countries of Southeast Asia, where only the most naïve citizen would expect to get something for nothing.

THE nature, degree and practice of corruption varies in the different lands of the region. It probably reached its apogee in the Philippines under ex-President Carlos P. Garcia, who retired at the end of 1961. Businessmen had to pay extra for licenses; directors of state agencies somehow "misplaced" funds; customs inspectors conspired with smugglers; and when asked to perform his duties, even the lowliest bureaucrat asked: *"Lagay muna?"*—almost literally, "Are you putting out?" Manila's papers were filled with reports of investigations, but few malefactors were ever arrested or convicted. Voted into office on promises to curb these excesses, successive presidents have found themselves stymied by the same problem: social custom and standards in the Philippines tend to work against honest civic action.

Philippine corruption is not merely a matter of enrichment. It descended in part from Spanish influence and Latin irreverence for finance. It also evolved from the autocracy of oriental society, in which ordinary people offer gifts to their superiors. And it is inextricably tied to the strong sense of family solidarity common throughout Asia. The successful man, whether in business or politics, is expected to support a vast collection of brothers, uncles, cousins and in-laws, and in the Philippines he must also extend favors to his *compadres,* a network of adopted kin. Challenged with the revelation that a high Filipino official was favoring his own wife's business, President Garcia said he saw "nothing wrong with a civil servant providing for his future."

CORRUPTION also is widespread among Thailand's officialdom. Petty functionaries expect remuneration for services rendered, and no businessman could expect to operate in Bangkok without pay-offs. But there is a certain propriety about graft in Thailand that makes it tolerable: a fixed sum to the proper person is like oil in the machine. Corruption in the Philippines—and in Burma and Indonesia as well—is unpredictable. Nobody is ever sure how many payments will have to be made, or to whom.

The extent to which corruption has hindered economic development in Southeast Asia is open to conjecture. There is no doubt that Indonesia loses significant amounts through the smuggling of copra and rubber out of its islands to northern Borneo and Singapore. It has been estimated that civic misbehavior in the Philippines during the Garcia administration deprived the government of some two billion pesos (about one billion dollars).

But neither corruption nor capricious leadership in themselves account for the lag in economic growth. In almost every country of Southeast Asia, there is a need for technical skills, tax reform and increased capital accumulation. Perhaps most important, governments have paid little attention to development of the countryside, where 75 per cent or more of their people live. In most areas, priorities have been given to transportation, communications and industry. Agriculture has been treated as a stepchild, and with obvious results. Light industry in the Philippines has expanded handsomely, but rice production has increased only slightly during the past decade. In South Vietnam, where victory in the current guerrilla war depends on winning the support of rural people, agriculture is allotted only a fraction of the state budget. Peasants are sullen and uncooperative, and as a farmer in Quangnam province explained, "Our heart is for the government that takes the least and gives the people happiness and abundance. We have not yet found that government."

Centered in their capitals and remote from the mass of their population, many governments of Southeast Asia are like heads without bodies. In ancient times, these lands had two associated classes, aristocrats and peasants. Today the division is between urban and rural folk, and there is scant connection between the two. Scarcely touched by modern influences, village existence is as simple as the immemorial wooden plow, and though rural life is changing slowly, its evolution is just perceptible.

THERE is no "typical" community of Southeast Asia. But a sample of rural stability in Thailand is Ban Sua Kham, "the village where tigers cross," which lies in the rich rice-growing plain above Bangkok. It is one of seven villages grouped together as a *tambon,* or commune.

Shaded by palms and eucalyptuses, Ban Sua Kham's 39 teakwood houses rise on stilts along the banks of the Chao Phraya. The river is the village's lifeline and its source of sustenance. At floodtime in the late spring it swells five feet or more, irrigating the paddy fields and covering them with the sediment that serves as fertilizer. Villagers bathe in the river, and it provides them with fish, their principal protein. It is the thoroughfare for shipping rice to market and for carrying water-borne peddlers down from the nearby town of Ayutthaya with such luxuries as coffee, needles and cotton. Nobody in Ban Sua Kham walks when he can use the river. Children adroitly paddle their fragile sampans upstream to school, and neighbors pull in for visits aboard a long, narrow, gaily painted river bus powered by an outboard motor.

LIKE all the villages of Thailand, Ban Sua Kham has a rudimentary kind of democracy. In the early '60s its *pu yai ban,* or headman, was a slight, wrinkled man of 60 named Tek Indra Udom, who was unanimously elected to the post more than 30 years earlier. By common consent he continued on in office. Tek was prosperous. He owned rice land which he rented to tenants for 25 per cent of their yield, and he had a monopoly on the sale of salt in the district. But his prominence was evident only in the size of his open-air, riverside grocery and his rambling house, whose walls were covered with calendars and portraits of uniformed officials who did him "favors," perhaps in exchange for bribes. Big-city Thais may drive Mercedeses and live in fancy houses, but in the countryside simplicity is a sign of virtue. Dressed in a faded sarong and undershirt, Tek never dreamed of displaying his wealth beyond perhaps wearing a wrist watch, or adorning his shirt pocket with a Parker 51 fountain pen.

When villagers come to a headman for help, they squat on the veranda of his place of business. They are offered betel nut, and as they chew they unfold their troubles modestly. Many problems are domestic. A husband complains that his wife has returned to her village. Yes, they had quarreled and he had beaten her, but now he is sorry and wants her back. And here is a farmer, brought in by his neighbors, who drank too much of the liquor known as *nam kao,* or "rice water," and disturbed the peace. The headman makes him promise to stay sober and puts him on parole. "Next time I'll call the police," he says without conviction, for there are no police in most villages.

Ban Sua Khan's most important crime within memory occurred more than ten years ago, when four robbers came down-river, held up a woman and tried to escape by boat. As they shoved off, the hefty housewife jumped onto their flimsy craft and capsized it, and the soaked criminals were easily dragged out of the water. Villagers talk of the incident as if it happened yesterday, and they are ever watchful for "bandits." Except for occasional cremations or weddings, there is, after all, no real excitement in Ban Sua Kham. In the dry season, an occasional brush fire arouses people, and the men supervise while women carry buckets of water from the river to protect their houses. Not long ago an affluent peasant went to Ayutthaya for a goiter operation, and while there he vowed that if he recovered he would send a theater company to Ban Sua Kham. Some weeks later a troupe of actors appeared, and for days they performed a *Likay* drama based on old legends of heroic kings and intriguing courtiers. Villagers discussed the play for months afterward.

FOR the farmer, 10 months of the year are daily drudgery and two months are total idleness. In May, as the heavy, dark monsoon clouds begin to cover the sky, he prepares his tools and sees his friendly Chinese middleman for cash to buy seeds, agreeing to repay the debt in rice. Early in June—on a day set by astrological calculation—plowing begins, and in the months that follow, the rice stalks must be transplanted and the paddy fields weeded, and the peasants must be constantly vigilant against the birds, rats and crabs that ravage crops. By February the rice is harvested and threshed. There is no mill at Ban Sua Kham, and the rice is taken away by Chinese buyers. If the peasant is solvent he can bargain to get a good price for his produce; if he is in debt, as most are, he must accept whatever is offered.

Farms in Ban Sua Kham vary in size from 10 to 40 acres. Vichien, a husky peasant in his early fifties, has 12 acres of land, two buffalo and a nephew who helps him. In a good year, when the rains fall on time and the weather holds, Vichien may harvest 22 tons of rice, worth perhaps $500 when prices are high. By Ban Sua Kham standards he is comfortable, and by Asian standards he is wealthy.

But Vichien is not ostentatious. His three children attend the village school, where they study reading, writing and arithmetic, and after the sixth grade they will go to work with their father. His wife cooks their meals of rice, boiled vegetables, fish curry and hot chili peppers, and when Vichien is farming she brings his food to the fields. They sleep on mats on the floor of their house, which creaks noisily to warn of intruders, and their only modern luxury is a transistor radio. In the evenings Vichien listens to music and Buddhist sermons from Bangkok.

LIKE the other farmers of Ban Sua Kham, Vichien is wary of change and sometimes worried by insecurity. There are no price supports in Thailand—or anywhere else in Southeast Asia—and a bad year could ruin him. Once, in the idle months between the harvest and new planting, he tried to make bamboo mats and baskets, but there was no market for these handicrafts, and he gave up. Another time he decided to raise poultry, and built chicken coops. But feed was too expensive and he lost money. Now he spends his spare time fishing. Properly irrigated, his land could yield two rice crops per year. That would, however, require more of an investment than Vichien and the other farmers of Ban Sua Kham could afford, and they do not expect any government help. "We are lucky when the government sends us some insecticide," says Vichien.

In a gradual way Ban Sua Kham is changing. A generation ago it took all day to paddle to Ayutthaya; now, with the outboard motor on the river bus, the town is an hour away. The radio has brought in the outside world. And education has changed. Once in the hands of Buddhist monks, teaching has been secularized in the commune school. It is broader and less severe, and many village leaders are somewhat perplexed. "In the old days," one of them remarked, "children were better disciplined. Now they can reason for themselves. Which is better?"

Young women pack pineapple in Kuala Lumpur. In Malaysia, light industry has attracted many workers from the farms.

A Wide Gulf between City and Farm

The people of the cities of Southeast Asia and the people of the rural villages live in sharply divided worlds. City dwellers live in a world of change with promises of a bright future. Villagers fish and farm with primitive tools and see no immediate hope of change. This division creates serious problems, for the city men who rule the new nations generally favor development of industry and trade and neglect agriculture, a situation the villagers bitterly resent.

SIDEWALK SHOP in a bazaar in Rangoon, Burma *(above)*, offers native and imported canned goods and many other commodities. Brisk trade has prompted merchants to push their booths out into the bazaar's streets.

FLOATING MARKET clutters a canal in Bangkok *(opposite)*, the merchants hawking vegetables and the fruits for which Thailand is famous. Bangkok has many miles of canals and much of the city's commerce is water-borne.

TIRELESS COOLIE in a wide sun hat ascends a narrow gangway *(left)*, balancing heavy baskets of rice at a large rice mill in Bangkok. Merchants make large profits buying rice cheaply from farmers and shipping it abroad.

BUSTLING CROWD in Saigon almost engulfs a fragile-looking girl who wears the traditional and elegant Vietnamese gown, called the *ao dai,* which is high-collared, sheath-slim and nearly ankle-length. Others wear the *non-la,* a conical straw hat used in Vietnam by both urban and rural women. Saigon has dozens of busy market

streets where exporters deal in tea and copra, rice and rubber. Despite the signs of a city at war—the men in uniform, the honky-tonk bars, even the sound of distant gunfire—Saigon's wide, tree-lined boulevards retain a measure of Parisian elegance, a legacy from the time the city was a wealthy center of the French colonial empire.

FISHING in the rivers and the seas is a major source of food and livelihood

SEAGOING OUTRIGGER manned by Indonesian Moslems coasts swiftly into Rembang, a port on the north coast of Java, after a fishing trip in the shallow Java Sea.

RIVER BOATS fish the waters of a stream near Hué, in South Vietnam. The nets, suspended from booms, are lowered into the river for a few minutes and then raised.

FARMING follows ancient, ritualistic patterns and often barely supports the people of the land

PEDAL-POWERED PUMP is used to irrigate a rice paddy in South Vietnam. Despite the country's political agony, the daily round of farm life has altered remarkably little.

RURAL FAMILY eats a noon meal in a farm hut in Vietnam *(opposite)*. Although the food is meager, Vietnamese wives take great pride in its meticulous preparation

COMMUNITY EFFORT raises a crude dam of earth and bamboo poles in an attempt to save a village's rice crop from being washed away by unseasonable rains.

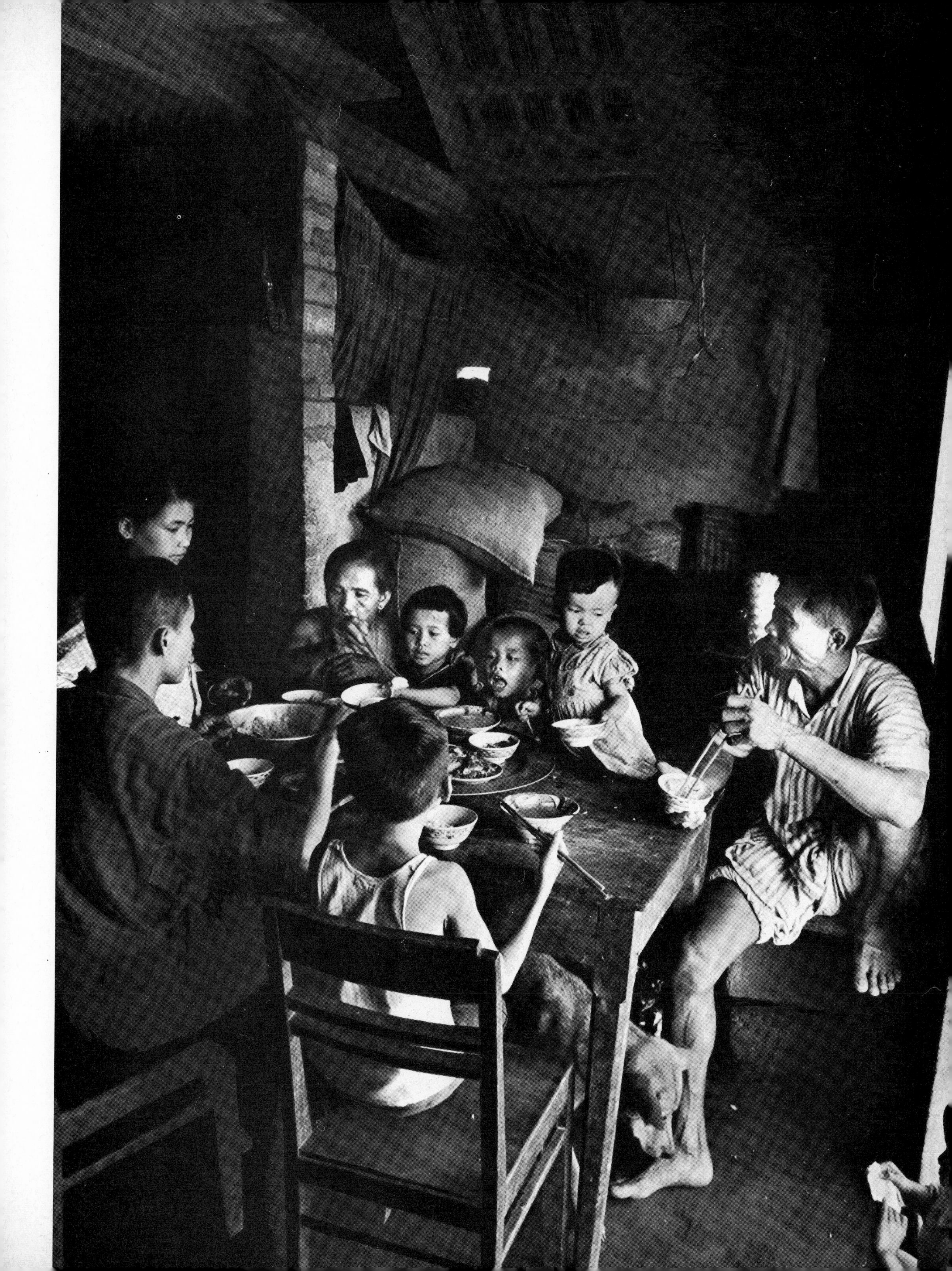

The greatest Burmese dancer of modern times, the late U Po Sein, instructs his son in one of the many positions used in Burma's stylized

dances, which re-enact stories drawn from the country's history.

6

A Past Alive in Ancient Arts

WARS, migrations, religious conversions, commercial convulsions and the constant corrosion of the tropics—all these have erased the ancient kingdoms of Southeast Asia. But the past still lives in the region's arts and culture. It thrives in the vibrant sculpture of Angkor Wat or the antic frown of a carved Burmese demon; in the boisterous drama of a Javanese puppet or the delicate grace of a Thai dancer. Even a woven bamboo basket from Malaya or a simple palm-frond dish from the Philippines reflects tradition.

The force of custom is overwhelming. Originality is of little importance in Southeast Asia; continuity is everything. As the American critic Faubion Bowers observed not long ago, the Asian artist "is fundamentally more interested in perfecting a single gesture transmitted to him by a long line of hereditary teachers than in discovering a new one, while his counterpart in the West can scarcely wait to escape the conservatory and spread his own wings according to the dictates of his own conscience."

Yet tradition flourishes in Southeast Asia because it is organic and fertile, and in its slow, imperceptible way it has evolved over thousands of years, bridging the past to the present. Thus archaic arts retain amazing vitality and immense popularity. Wandering Laotian storytellers combine antique myths with parables of war and trouble that, in Laos' present plight, sound as timely as news dispatches. Philippine song-plays, called zarzuelas, mix lachrymose melodrama with lively political verve.

IN the Sunda districts of Java, the wayfaring *dalang* carries his chest of equipment into a village and erects his screen before blazing torches, and from midnight until dawn his buffalohide puppets perform *wayang kulit,* a shadow play with moral lessons. As in American horse operas, good and evil *wayang* characters are easily recognizable, and courage, loyalty and refinement always triumph. The message never changes, no matter what the plot. The story may tell of Arjuna, the ascetic whom the god Shiva tempted with beautiful nymphs, an 11th Century Javanese tale derived from a far older Indian legend. The *dalang* may recount episodes from the venerable Indian *Ramayana,* which is as old as the *Iliad* and, like Homer's epic, tells of a beauty's abduction and the furious war to rescue her. The spectators sit enraptured as the *dalang* spins out the stories they all know so well, laughing as he improvises a moment of humor, trembling as he flashes to the excitement of battle, sighing at a love poem from the *Mahabharata,* its Sanskrit origin lost beyond memory but its strophes as romantic as ever:

> *With the moon of her countenance, and the delight of the movements of its brows, and the sweetness of the words tripping from her mouth, with her charm and her soft loveliness, she seemed to be challenging the moon as she walked along.*

As alive as the drama is Indonesia's traditional dance, and in no other land of Southeast Asia is it given such official encouragement. President Sukarno rants regularly against "the madness of rock and roll" and "the din of swing and jazz," but he melts at the sight of a curled finger or a gracefully arched neck, and he expects visiting foreign dignitaries to do the same. A few years ago he subjected Soviet Premier Khrushchev to more than a week of daily performances. Khrushchev was visibly surfeited, but more sensitive spectators of Indonesian dancing have been enraptured and disarmed by its diversity and skill.

One could probably watch Indonesian dancers for months without seeing the same spectacle twice. This enormous variety mirrors the cultural complexity of an archipelago comprised of some 3,000 islands, in which close to 100 million people speak more than 150 different dialects and languages. Styles in Java range from the explosive mask dances of the Sunda region to the gentle, passive, almost contemplative motions of palace performers in Solo and Jogjakarta, where sultanic courts still survive. Nearly every tiny area of Sumatra has its choreographic particularity, and each of the outer islands offers a different kind of ritual dance, some primitive and aboriginal. Above all this field of fragments is Bali, the tiny island of two million people that Prime Minister Nehru of India has called "the world's morning, its last paradise."

YET for all its apparent pristine charm, Bali is changing. Girls whose mothers unashamedly exposed their breasts may now wear tight bodices, paint their fingernails and ride bicycles. Indonesian government officials, nettled by the island's distinctiveness, bombard Bali with nationalist slogans of *revolusi* and *sosialisme;* and Communist agents, playing on economic discontent, organize its disappointed youth. But in this last outpost of Hinduism in Southeast Asia—the only large one in the world outside India—artistry is still vital. It thrives in ornate flower offerings to the spirits; in the terraced rice fields rising on hill slopes fringed with palms; in the elaborate cremation of a deceased ruler, whose soul is delivered to *Sang Hyang Widhi-Wasa,* the Creator, while priests chant and a red paper dragon 300 feet long bursts into flame.

Among Southeast Asia's plastic artists, the Balinese are foremost in their mixture of traditional and modern techniques, creating paintings as lively in their detail as ancient temple friezes, and soft white satinwood carvings of elongated or massive figures in calm repose. Each village of Bali has its cultural guild, and almost every Balinese has some artistic avocation, from dancing to playing one or another of the xylophones, gongs and flutes of the gamelan orchestra. The range of Balinese dance themes is astonishing. The performers may dance ageless passages from the *Ramayana,* fire dances, dagger dances and the contorted *Ketjak,* or Monkey Dance. There are trancelike movements of celestial nymphs nearly hypnotized by the music, and lavish solos improvised from basic gestures as creatively as a composer might construct a string quartet from a folk tune.

A MORE subtle, stable people than the Balinese, the Thais have also developed their culture carefully and consciously over the years. Though they have less money and leisure time nowadays, Thai noblemen have always patronized—and often participated in—the arts. King Rama I, who founded the present dynasty in the late 18th Century, made his palace a cultural center. He composed a Thai version of the *Ramayana,* called the *Ramakian,* neatly adapting the Hindu epic to his Buddhist faith by scissoring out the religious passages. To encourage dance training, he revised the ancient collection of basic figures to include movements like "The Bee's Caress" or "Fish Playing in the Ocean." And for dancers to practice these motions, Rama I created a *pas de deux* between a clumsy demon and a beautiful girl "to show how different are the styles of a person who can dance and a person who cannot." Rama's curriculum is still observed in Thai dancing schools.

Before they can put on their ornate, brocaded costumes, pointed crowns and grotesque masks, Thai dancers—like Cambodian, Javanese, Burmese and other performers—must go through years of rigorous muscular preparation. They must practice bending their hands back until their fingers, arching like the petals of a flower, touch their forearms. They must double-joint their elbows, and loosen their wrists until they can affect the profile of a swan with their hands. Some dancers have even been known to have their bones broken and reset to achieve difficult limb movements. In contrast to the western ballet, with its smooth, supple gestures, oriental dancing has a grace that tends more toward angular poses. Whether on the stage or on temple façades, Asian dancers often seem chiseled in stone.

Tradition has also given continuing vitality to Southeast Asia's handicrafts. Nearly every region produces its distinctive textiles, often made by farmers in the hiatus between harvest and planting. Filipinos create fragile fabrics out of pineapple fibers, and Indonesians manufacture their cotton batik, hand-dyed with geometric patterns or birds, butterflies and flowers. Cambodians, Javanese and Malays work intricate designs in silver; Burmese and Vietnamese artisans make colorful lacquerware; and everywhere, bamboo, palm leaves, banana fronds and assorted reeds are transformed into a gay variety of functional bags, baskets, plates and mats. Perhaps nothing reflects Southeast Asia's diversity so well as peasant hats, which range from the simple cones of Vietnam to the brightly hued hexagons of Borneo's hill tribes.

CONTEMPORARY painting and sculpture are still undeveloped in Southeast Asia, yet ancient plastic arts are coming to life again in discoveries by serious connoisseurs and archeologists. Few wooden artifacts have survived the damp, destructive tropical heat, but the jungles and deltas of the area are constantly yielding up brilliant pieces of pottery, jewelry and religious images in stone and bronze. With their casual disregard for history and their belief in the impermanence of things, native people are rather oblivious to these relics of the past. A good Buddhist, for example, earns more "merit" for building a new temple than for restoring an old one, and concern for old art has been stimulated mostly by Westerners and westernized Asians.

Discerning collectors played a big part in arousing artistic interest in the region, although some were excessively enthusiastic. The great critic and novelist André Malraux, France's Minister of Cultural Affairs, was so acquisitive during his youthful years in the Far East that he was arrested trying to spirit *objets d'art* out of Cambodia. His novel *The Royal Way* is partly based on this experience. Other art lovers in these lands have displayed similar avidity. A German engineer living in Thailand some years ago reputedly acquired a large and admirable collection of Buddha heads, which he had struck from their bodies to make shipment home simpler and less costly. Most governments in Southeast Asia now have passed laws that are intended to control the export of such valuable antiques, but smuggling remains widespread throughout the area.

STYLIZED TRIO, these three puppets combat evil and supply humor in the *wayang*, or shadow plays, performed for centuries in Indonesia.

Much of the growing fascination with Thai art has resulted from the conscientious collecting and scholarship of Americans. A former New York architect and army officer, James H.W. Thompson, almost singlehandedly revived the country's traditional silk industry by teaching native craftsmen how to use European dyes. Diligently rummaging the countryside—until his disappearance into the Malaysian jungle in 1967—Thompson assembled an impressive collection of antiques and made his home into a splendid museum. Another former American officer, Alexander B. Griswold, has extensively researched and catalogued the historical styles of ancient Thai sculpture and architecture. Indiana University introduced Thai art to the United States in 1960-1961 when it initiated a touring exhibition of statues, paintings, manuscripts, ceramics and other pieces.

Far more impressive, however, have been the efforts of European experts in restoring and studying the great Southeast Asian civilizations of the past. It was western science, esthetic interest and sheer hard work that breathed new life into the region's artistic legacies, and bestowed upon these lands the past glories they had themselves largely ignored. British scholarship, for example, was mainly responsible for uncovering the story of Pagan, the great Burman kingdom whose temples still stand like sleepy sentinels, gazing out upon the winding Irrawaddy.

Southwest of Mandalay, Pagan was most probably founded in the 9th or 10th Century, not long after the Burmans roamed down from southern China. They conquered the Mons, who had settled in Lower Burma centuries before, and from them acquired the Buddhist canon, as well as the arts and skills of India. Equipped with this superior culture, the Burmans then embarked upon an orgy of building. They constructed the enormous Ananda temple, whose gilded spire rises 163 feet above the ground. They also raised the cylindrical Shwezigon, which is supposed to contain a tooth of the Gautama Buddha himself, but which, in that curious oriental marriage of superstition and formal religion, also displays a pantheon of Burma's 37 *nats*, or principal animistic spirits. In the 250 years of the Pagan kingdom, thousands of other temples were built. None of them, however, matches the greater works of Java and Cambodia. "One feels," says the British scholar Reginald le May, "that the Pagan kings

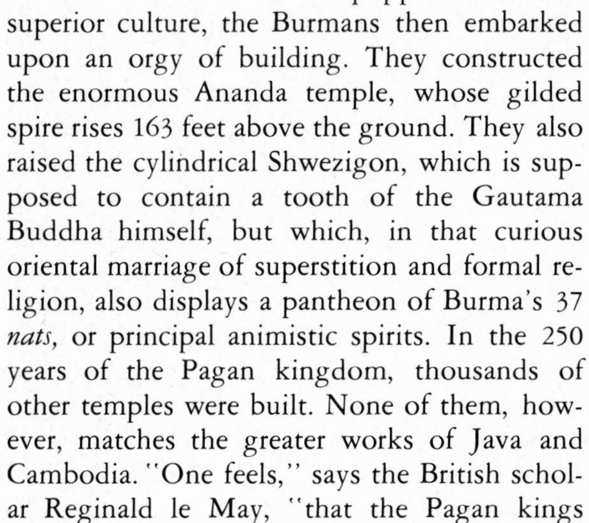

wanted to build something grand and splendid without quite knowing what to build or how to build it."

If their quality is not the highest, the vast panorama of Pagan's temples testifies to the fervor and power of a culture that proclaimed its greatness in quantity. Archeologists have counted 2,190 temples within the capital's 25 square miles. Burman folklore claims, however, that at its peak the kingdom had 4,446,733 temples of various sizes. Such fantastic superlatives run through all the old royal chronicles. A king is reported to command 36 million soldiers, maintain 3,000 concubines and eat 300 plates of curry daily. The king is invariably pious, wise, brave and just, and he sits upon a gem-encrusted throne of gold while "the maiden daughters of many princes, adorned with jewels and holding white parasols, shall attend him." In war he rides "a noble steed bred of the clouds, that shines like the noonday sun," and the longer his title, the greater his glory. One ruler of Pagan, the chronicles say, was called *Sri Tribhuwanadityadhammarajarajadhirajaparamiswarabalacakkrawar,* which in addition to other things means "Supreme King of Kings, Overlord and Mighty Universal Monarch." Eventually Pagan strained itself to exhaustion, and when Kublai Khan's fierce Mongol cavalrymen rode into the region late in the 13th Century, the kingdom collapsed.

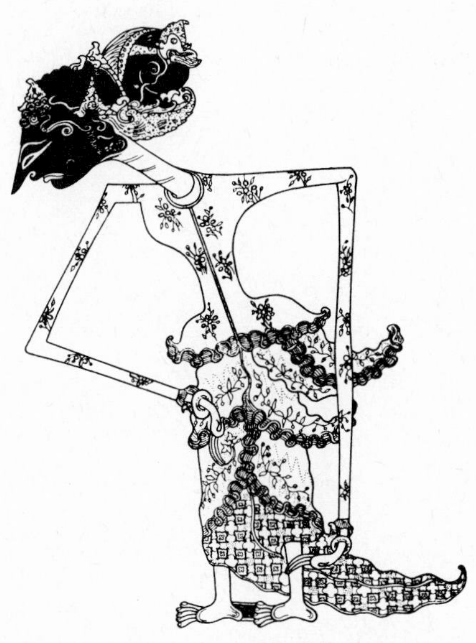

ANGULAR LADY postures in a *wayang* play based on an Indian epic. *Wayang* shows contain dozens of characters.

In Java, Dutch archeologists borrowed from the method used in reconstructing the Acropolis. Called "anastylosis," it consists of taking ruins apart, numbering the pieces and putting them back together again, like solving an incredibly complex jigsaw puzzle. Patiently these scientists rebuilt much of Java's former magnificence, including the enormous Buddhist pyramid of Borobudur, near Jogjakarta. Unlike the temples of Pagan, which mainly reflect a state's wealth and piety, Borobudur is in itself an architectural and sculptural masterpiece.

Looking calmly across Java's Kedu plateau and hazy hills beyond, Borobudur is believed to date back to the Eighth Century, when the Sailendra Dynasty had attained the height of its power in the region. Built around a hill, it is a stupa, or pagoda—479 feet square at its base and 150 feet high—of six terraces, a spire rising from the topmost of them. Some 400 images of Buddha adorn the edifice, all sitting cross-legged with only their *mudras,* or hand gestures, varying to indicate their different moods. The temple's galleries contain more than three miles of bas-reliefs illustrating Buddhist texts and, almost incidentally, showing scenes from ancient Javanese life.

Since 1814, when it was uncovered amid jungle vegetation by a British surveyor, Borobudur has been discussed and interpreted by Asian and western scholars. It has been described often as "the upper stages of the cosmic mountain," a symbol which lies at the root of much of Buddhist and Hindu ritual.

The idea of the temple-mountain arose originally in the Middle East, and passed through India to the Southeast Asians. To all these peoples, life was governed by a mystical link between the microcosm and the macrocosm, between man and the universe. Unlike Westerners, who believe that man's destiny lies not in the stars but in himself, Asians have long been persuaded that every aspect of their existence is determined by cosmic forces—the movements of stars, planets and the sun. To find harmony with these forces, they created a mythical model of the universe. This was the magic mountain—Meru—which was the center, pivot and axis of the universe, and within which all things had their ordained and preappointed position.

Just as this concept of a harmonious, ordered universal macrocosm governed every detail of life—from political conduct to procreation—so it inspired art and architecture. The Indianized builders of Southeast Asia held their mirror up to faith, not nature. They were attempting to express not man's power over the earth, but man's submission to the gods. Greek columns and Gothic cathedral towers are vertical. The structures of Asia also rise toward the sky, but their pattern is horizontal. They are laid out in rectangular or square enclosures, mounting tier by tier in a gently ascending pyramid. Man looks up at the lofty spires of the cathedral of Chartres; heaven looks down on Borobudur.

Translated into stone, the philosophy of the magic mountain reached its daring, breathtaking apogee in the extraordinary kingdom of Angkor. Sprawled over 10,000 acres, more than 20 of the capital's major monuments emerge from the lush Cambodian jungle like some terrestrial Atlantis surrounded by a sea of green foliage. To local natives, descendants of the Khmers who built the temples, Angkor was "the work of giants." The French naturalist Henri Mouhot, who stumbled upon the ruins in 1860, considered them "far more grandiose than anything built in the heyday of Greek or Roman art."

LABORING in malarial jungles, with little modern equipment, cutting away thick tree roots and tangled vines, French archeologists spent more than half a century rebuilding Angkor, and their work still continues. Their studies of its origin and growth were prodigious. They trace its beginnings back to the turn of the Ninth Century, when Southeast Asia was in the full ferment of Indian influence. A Cambodian prince, exiled in Java, somehow returned to his homeland and settled on the northern shore of the great inland sea of Tonle Sap. In 802 he proclaimed himself King Jayavarman II of sovereign Kambuja (Cambodia) and founded an empire that was to last more than six centuries and spread its power as far west as Burma.

To assert his peerless independence and superiority over all earthly beings, Jayavarman conceived of himself as a devaraja, a god-king, whose divinity was sponsored by the Great Shiva and whose symbol was the phallic *linga*. This stone *linga* stood for prosperity, fertility and power, and its sanctuary was the summit of the temple-mountain, in which the king's magic soul survived after his death. In egocentric drives to immortalize their spirits, Angkor's succession of kings all tried to outdo one another in the magnificence of their mausoleums. To a large extent the tremendous burden of building these funerary temples eventually wrecked the country. The effort nevertheless bequeathed a concentrated display of rare artistic brilliance.

JUST as organisms became more complex through life's evolution, so Angkor's temples grew more elaborate and complicated as time went by. In the early years of the Ninth Century, Angkor's sculpture was stylized and simple. The tiny, charming temple of Banteai Srei, erected about a century later, displays exquisitely balanced façades of refined sculpted figures—lovely nymphs, gods and demons enacting the epic *Mahabharata*. The later Bayon temple, its huge stone faces half-smiling, is mature and meditative; its builder was a Buddhist.

For sheer grandeur, however, nothing exceeds Angkor Wat, the great temple completed in the early decades of the 12th Century. In this majestic edifice, the civilization of the Khmers reached its pinnacle. Colossal, regal, awesome, vital—all the adjectives apply, and none is entirely descriptive. Angkor Wat is 10 times the size of Canterbury Cathedral, yet almost all of its stones are decorated with affectionate care. Perhaps inadvertently, the contrast between its immensity and detail again symbolizes the span between lowly man and infinite universe. It is "the navel of the earth and the gateway of heaven," and its carved panels flow with excitement. There are nimble dancing girls and gruesome gods, fierce battle melees and scenes of the Hindu underworld as terrifying as the hell feared by medieval Europeans. Representing the Khmer king, the god Vishnu cavorts in different guises, allegorically guiding his subjects. And like a never-ending film, the façades unfold the militant heroism, religious romanticism and intimate reality of a people lost in time but alive in stone.

THE builders of Angkor were originally woodworkers who carved with the same technique in laterite, a local gray stone that is soft when quarried but hardens in the air and sunlight. Using only crude instruments, they performed surveying miracles, such as laying out a three-mile moat that runs off course only half an inch. It is perhaps more of a miracle, however, that their buildings ever rose from the ground at all, for they were inadequate architects. They seemed to consider construction a boring necessity, to be achieved quickly in order to provide the façades for their dramatic decorations, and the temples abound with evidence of hasty, shoddy workmanship.

Like most Asians, the Khmers never learned the secret of the true arch, and they improvised gloomy, corbeled vaults rather than spacious chambers. They irrationally tried to adapt wood-building methods to stone construction, ignoring such problems as proper jointing and weight distribution. Essentially they were artists rather than technicians, dedicated to transforming a cosmological idea into a stone monument covered with dynamic arabesques. They succeeded brilliantly despite themselves.

The heady resplendence of Angkor's art was matched by the capital's rich, giddy social life. The anonymous Khmer rice farmer lived in daily drudgery, as the Cambodian peasant does today. But the aristocracy of priests and courtiers sparkled with wealth. A single sanctuary might contain 10 tons of gold and silver, thousands of pearls and hundreds of silk beds. The 13th Century Chinese traveler Chou Ta-kuan, who spent a year in Angkor, has described the affluent hullabaloo of its lake port, where Indian and Chinese merchant ships brought in cargoes of gold, rice paper, glass and porcelain to exchange for copper and tin, rhinoceros horn, and highly prized kingfisher wings to crown Chinese brides.

Near the royal palace, recounted Chou Ta-kuan, were the stalls of artisans—goldsmiths and weavers, woodworkers and lacquerers—and within the sumptuous court lived the king, his five wives and thousands of concubines. The mighty monarch wore robes of richly flowered brocade, a necklace of pearls, and bracelets of gold on his wrists and ankles, but went barefoot. When he went forth on state occasions, his procession comprised cavalry, handmaidens, ministers and princes, wives and concubines—and finally, protected by guards and surrounded by the white parasols that denoted his rank, came the king himself, standing erect on a gold-tusked elephant and bearing his sword of office. As the pennants and banners and music passed by, the people touched the ground with their foreheads, raising them only "when the sound of the conches died away."

IN the end this glory was self-defeating. Dedicated solely to the god-king, the kingdom collapsed under the weight of its own self-centered magnificence. Khmer culture deeply influenced the Thais, who conquered Angkor in its weakest hour. Nevertheless, Angkor's artistic genius sent forth no durable values to the world. Angkor's French curator, Bernard-Philippe Groslier, compares this ancient Cambodian civilization to Egypt, Japan and the Inca Empire, whose splendid cultures did not transcend their own frontiers in the way that those of Greece, Rome, India and China inspired other peoples. But if Angkor remains outside the mainstream of universal experience, it is still unique. "Where it is unsurpassable," concludes Groslier, "is in its size, the harmony of those enormous structures, the feeling of what may be called urbanism. . . . And because the temple-mountain was constructed out of space and time, it still dominates the one and has defied the other."

In self-induced hysterical trances, a group of Balinese cut themselves with daggers during the most violent of their native dances. They

Gestures in Flesh and Bronze

The artistic heritage of the countries of Southeast Asia is rich in both dance and sculpture. Many of the dances tell tales of gods and heroes drawn from the great Hindu epics like the *Ramayana*, their themes dating back to the

believe they are warding off the evil magic of the Queen of the Witches. Afterward friends treat the cuts and put red flowers in them.

time when Hinduism first spread to the region. They are still performed today, along with dances reflecting everyday concerns. Sculpture, too, developed early, often giving shape and meaning, as did the dances, to religious figures. Most triumphant in their cool, formal perfection are the serene statues of the Buddha which abound wherever that contemplative faith followed Hinduism, and especially in countries like Thailand where Buddhism still flourishes.

GRACEFUL RITUAL characterizes the Legong dance of Bali which is performed by young girls carefully schooled in the subtle, sinuous gestures that have remained virtually unchanged for centuries

WAITING to dance *(above),* four girls make last-minute adjustments in their robes and make-up. Their bodies are tightly girdled with many yards of heavy cloth, which is then covered by gorgeous silks embellished with gold.

PREPARING for the *Legong* dance, a young performer *(left)* patiently waits for her hair to be arranged. The white dot on her forehead, the three near her temple and the painted eyebrows are the traditional dancer's make-up

GESTURING, a young girl holds her hand palm outward in one of the classic poses of the Balinese dance. Many of the dances of Bali consist of intricate movements which require muscular control and physical endurance.

SCULPTURE portraying saviors and demons reflects the deep, ever-present concern with religion and the spirit

INTENT APPRENTICE at a wood-carving school in Java *(left)* shapes part of a screen which will include the demon's face he has carved *(foreground)*. Some Indonesian grotesque carvings are thought to ward off evil spirits.

SERENE FACE of a Buddha *(opposite)* which dates from the 15th Century shows the long ears and curled hair associated in the East with heroes. The painted features and bluish patina enhance the look of unearthly repose.

LEANING STATUE shows the Buddha pressing a footprint into the earth as a reminder of him and his teachings. The indentations in the bronze pedestal represent footprints left by previous incarnations of the Buddha.

GLEAMING BUDDHA, cast in the 14th Century and covered with gold *(opposite)*, lifts a hand to dispel fear. The Buddha's body is said to have been incandescent, and the flames on top of the head symbolize his fiery energy.

LOFTY DOME tops a Buddhist shrine on the outskirts of Mandalay in Burma. Shrines like this attract many pilgrims, who make offerings of food and flowers and meditate on the rules of self-discipline taught by Buddha.

7

Many Shapes of the Spirit

LIKE the bee drawing honey from many flowers, argues an oriental proverb, the wise man accepts the essence of different scriptures. This tolerant, eclectic attitude pervades Southeast Asia, and it is reflected in the complex and confusing variety of the region's spiritual beliefs and practices.

Islam, Buddhism, Christianity, Confucianism, Hinduism—all these flourish throughout the area, coexisting peacefully with lesser cults and sects, such as the weird Moslem offshoots in Java or the Cao Dai of Vietnam, whose saints include Victor Hugo and Joan of Arc. And in one way or another, to varying degrees and under assorted guises, each religion consorts with a giddy array of myth and magic. Interest is widespread in astrology, phrenology and palmistry; in ghosts and phantoms; in occult compounds of herbs and salves; in a formidable and often puzzling pantheon of good and malevolent spirits which must be wooed, appeased, nourished or frightened away.

Seemingly heretical, this intrusion of superstition into formal faith responds to traditional Asian needs and feelings. The rational Westerner distinguishes between the spiritual and the physical; he separates God and Caesar. In the Orient, with its conception of a coherent universe, all forms of life are unified: the earth to the heavens, the real to the imaginary, the natural to the supernatural. Almost everywhere in Southeast Asia, religious orthodoxy is more an abstract ideal than a reality.

With some 85 million Moslems—about 90 per cent of the population—Indonesia is the largest Islamic land in the world. But the fiery faith of the Prophet Mohammed is almost unrecognizable in the archipelago. Here Islam has inspired none of the brilliant architecture of North Africa or the Middle East. Visitors to Java are proudly shown ancient Hindu and Buddhist temples, and in Malaysia, where Islam is also strong, the principal Moslem-looking building—complete with Moorish arches and turnip-topped towers—is the railroad station in Kuala Lumpur, the capital. Most Islamic schools and places of worship in these lands are simple, and the only mosque of any grandeur in all Southeast Asia looms with grotesque prominence in the tiny, oil-rich British protectorate of Brunei, on the northern coast of Borneo. Built a few years ago at a cost of $2.5 million by Sultan Sir Omar Ali Saifuddin Wasa'dul Khairi Waddin, Knight Commander of St. Michael and St. George—and named for himself—it has electric incense burners and an elevator to run the muezzin up the minaret from which he calls the faithful to prayer through a loud-speaker.

NOR is there much evidence in these countries of the fervor that sped the word of Allah over the continents. Truly oriental in its passivity, Islam in the Far East provoked no bitter, bloody feuds. Today, it enforces no rigorous codes of conduct such as Moslems must bear in some Arab countries. Much of this moderation derived from the way Islam developed in the Orient. It did not have far-reaching effects upon Malaya and Indonesia until the late 13th Century, more than 600 years after Islam's birth in the Middle East, and in the long passage through Persia and India it lost a good deal of its vigor. More important, it was carried into the region by peaceful Indian merchants more concerned with commerce than proselytizing. Asian princes were attracted to the new religion because its adherents exuded an aura of wealth and prosperity, and peasants liked its message of man's equality before God. But none of these early converts felt compelled to obey its precepts rigidly.

ALMOST casual in its growth, Islam remained relaxed in its behavior. Moslems in Malaysia, for example, retained the Brahmanic rites they had performed previously, inserting prayers to Allah into Hindu incantations, and syncretizing this novel monotheism with ancient animistic habits. To this day, Mohammed's tenets have not replaced village law in Indonesia. The Minangkabaus of central Sumatra consider themselves fervent Moslems, yet for centuries they have passed legacies down through the female line, ignoring Islam's dictum of male supremacy. Many traditional Moslem practices are also not observed. Elsewhere in the Indonesian archipelago, women are not veiled, and polygamy is rare—although couples take advantage of Islam's easy divorce opportunities. For every two marriages in Indonesia each year, one is repudiated. In highly un-Moslem fashion, however, wives are as free to initiate divorces as their husbands.

If its theological impact was weak, Islam exerted a strong secular influence on Southeast Asia. In its way, it brought to a part of the region a radical, humanitarian outlook. As Christianity had in the West, Islam endowed the common man with a sense of his individual value. He might be socially inferior to princes and chieftains, but there was now a spiritual lift to his life. And his relation to other Moslems gave him a new feeling of solidarity that was, in time, to play a significant role in the rise of nationalism.

Islam also brought modern ideas to Indonesia. Inspired by reformist trends in Egypt, Indonesian scholars tried to bring Islam into harmony with contemporary thought during the early years of the 20th Century. They created the Muhammadiyya movement, which

SOME RECURRING SYMBOLS

In Southeast Asian temples these four figures occur repeatedly. To Hindus the serpent Naga symbolizes the life-giving power of water; to Buddhists he is associated with the Buddha, who tradition says was protected by a serpent. The Garuda represents the divine eagle, symbol of the sky. He is also the vehicle for Vishnu, a god in the Hindu trinity. The elephant, often observed guarding Hindu temples, also reflects a tradition that the Buddha was a six-tusked elephant in an early incarnation. At right is the monkey-god, companion to Vishnu.

frankly copied the tactics of Christian missionaries. It crusaded against sermons in Arabic, which nobody understood, and its *muballighs*, or propagandists, established schools, hospitals, orphanages, libraries, scout troops and a women's association. In the postwar years of independence, the Muhammadiyya was a potent force in all domains but one—politics. But it had fertilized the soil from which Moslem political movements could spring, and until Indonesia's president restricted political activity in 1960, religious groups were among the most powerful organizations in the country. In addition, fanatic Moslem insurgents like the members of Darul Islam, which advocates a theocratic state, have waged guerrilla warfare against the government for years.

While discouraging Moslem politics, Indonesia has not hesitated to use religion as an instrument of policy, and the banners of Islam are often waved to rally the people to different causes. Chosen Moslem spokesmen preached the liberation of nearby Dutch New Guinea as a kind of jihad, or holy war. In a speech in 1961, Dr. Ruslan Abdulgani, the former vice chairman of the government's Supreme Advisory Council, proclaimed that Islam was opposed to usury and therefore incompatible with capitalism. But Moslem teachings were not inconsistent with Marxism, he explained, and he called upon Islamic centers to help propagate Indonesian-style socialism.

Little of such worldliness characterizes Buddhism, which is far more deeply ingrained among its adherents in Southeast Asia. Observed by some 60 million Burmese, Thais, Cambodians, Laotians and Vietnamese, Buddhism is less a formal religion than an intensely individual ethic, and an understanding of its precepts is essential to a comprehension of

Southeast Asia. It offers no deity, no dogma to be taken on faith, no doctrine of immortality, no concept of divine revelation. In essence, Buddhism is a search for truth and enlightenment, goals to be attained by observing dharma, the all-embracing principles of righteousness expounded by the Buddha.

Buddhism is not native to Southeast Asia. It burgeoned in India more than 25 centuries ago, originating as a sort of protestant reformation. Hinduism was the subcontinent's dominant religion at the time, and it was in a state of decay. Caste barriers had solidified, and the members of the leading caste, the priestly Brahmins, imparted little to the people but hollow, incomprehensible rituals. Dissatisfied with this atrophied faith, thousands of religious rebels erupted—skeptics, atheists, agnostics, nihilists and materialists, all disputing among themselves in an amazing atmosphere of philosophical ferment. It was into this fulminating atmosphere that a Hindu prince was born in the foothills of the Himalayas. The son of the chieftain of the Gautama clan of the Shakya tribes, the boy was called Siddhartha.

LIKE the other young aristocrats of his day, Siddhartha learned archery and riding, and as a member of the warrior caste he was taught the arts of war. In time he married, became a good husband and father, and led a happy, prosperous life. But one day, when he was 29, Siddhartha walked into the streets of his city and saw an old man; on another day he saw a sick man; on the third day he saw a dead man. He returned to his palace to reflect on these sights. As pious tradition tells it, he was "troubled, ashamed and disgusted," and he resolved to seek out the nature of birth, old age, sickness, sorrow and impurity.

Leaving his wife and small son, Siddhartha went forth to find the truth. First he tried the way of the ascetic, lying on thorns, sleeping among rotting corpses, and living on seeds and grass. But six years of this self-mortification taught him nothing. He went to Bodh-gaya, in central Bihar province, and there he sat down in the shade of a *bodhi,* or wild fig tree, determined not to move until the answer to his quest came to him. After 49 days of meditation, Gautama Siddhartha found truth, and became the Buddha, the Enlightened One.

Himself a Hindu, the Buddha inherited and accepted certain ancient Hindu beliefs. One of these was the concept of metempsychosis: not exactly the reincarnation of an individual soul in another body, but the rebirth in another guise—animal or human—of one's karma, the score of merits and demerits acquired by good or bad conduct during a lifetime. Another was the view of the world as a place of ignorance and sadness, from which wise men should seek release. In his vision under the *bodhi* tree, the Buddha saw the current of life pass before him —birth and death, grief and joy, pain and peace. And in that stream he found the cause of human sorrow. It lay in rebirth, which forever replenished the cycle of human suffering.

The Buddha believed that rebirth could be avoided if a man followed a life of perfect justice and constant patience and kindness, renouncing all desire for worldly pleasures. He could then attain that release called nirvana. In the ancient Indian language of Sanskrit, nirvana means "final emancipation." In Buddhist thought, however, it does not signify an end of existence. Nirvana is, rather, an intangible, everlasting state of peace—"indescribable, inconceivable, ineffable." As the Buddha himself affirmed it: "Nirvana is bliss."

THE Buddha spent the next 45 years of his life wandering through northern India, talking, lecturing and relating parables that contained the core of his teachings. At the basis of his philosophy, there were the Four Noble Truths: suffering is universal; its cause is craving, or selfish desire; its cure is the elimination of desire; and the way to eliminate craving is to take the middle way between sensuality and asceticism. To find the middle way, the Buddha explained, man had to follow the Noble Eightfold Path—right knowledge, right intention, right speech, right conduct, right means of livelihood, right effort, right mindfulness and right concentration. When his disciples asked him to define right speech and action more clearly, the Buddha formulated Five Moral Rules—not to kill, steal or lie; to abstain from illicit sexual pleasure and to avoid alcohol.

Just as complex religions evolved from the basic teachings of Jesus, so a vast canonical literature grew out of the Buddha's sermons. Fundamental to Buddhist thought is the idea of impermanence. There is neither soul nor self; everything changes. Even the Gautama Buddha himself was not unique. He was not divine; there were many Buddhas before him, and many Buddhas will follow.

WITHIN 200 years after the Buddha's death, there were no fewer than 18 formalized interpretations of his creed. One of them, called the Mahayana, or Greater Vehicle, has been likened to Mediterranean Christianity in its profusion of relics, rosaries, liturgies and Bodhisattvas, saintlike candidates for future Buddhahood. This dramatic, colorful form of Buddhism spread north into Tibet, Mongolia, Japan and China, and the Chinese carried it to Vietnam. Another Buddhist branch, the Hinayana, or Lesser Vehicle, remained more fundamental, and from southern India and Ceylon it passed into Burma, Thailand and the rest of Southeast Asia.

Through the centuries, Buddhism developed firm foundations, and a measure of its power is obvious not only in the art and architecture it inspired, but in the numbers of its devout followers. In Thailand today, there are some 20,000 monasteries and more than 150,000 regular monks. Every year more than 50,000 young men temporarily leave their jobs to become 90-day monks. When his time to serve came a few years ago, even Thailand's King Bhumibol Adulyadej shaved his head, donned the three parts of his orange robe, and went into a monastery with begging bowl, umbrella, needle, razor and bit of cloth to strain tea lest he inadvertently swallow a live bug and thereby contravene the Buddhist sanction against killing.

The sangha, or brotherhood of Buddhist monks, attracts as varied an assortment of men as any priestly order. Some are lazy, others are dedicated, and often a prominent politician or general will spend his retirement as a monk, perhaps to gain merit to make up for the evil acts of his professional career. In Thailand, Burma or Cambodia, the Buddhist monk's life is simple, studious and celibate. He sleeps on a straw mat in a dormitory behind his temple, rising at dawn to recite a prayer in Pali, the liturgical language of Buddhism, thanking the Buddha for showing him the path to nirvana and reflecting on the impermanence of all existence. Before 6 a.m. he goes out to beg, taking a prescribed route laid out for him by the temple abbot. Monks are not openly thankful for the food they receive; on the contrary, it is the donor who is grateful, for in giving he gains some of the merit that will determine his state after rebirth.

Before noon, the monk will have eaten his two daily meals of rice and vegetables. He devotes his afternoon to studying Buddhist law, debating the finer points of the canon, or discussing tales from the Jatakas, which tell of the many lives of the Buddha. Some monks have hobbies and a few of the older and wiser ones dispense advice to villagers. Many officiate at funerals or teach children, but these Buddhist clergymen are not priests who lead prayers or hear confessions. Each Buddhist, monk or layman, must find the truth within himself, as did the Buddha, and each knows the paths of righteousness to follow. "The Buddha can only tell you the way," says the scripture. "It is for you yourself to make the effort."

EMBODYING the virtues of charity, tolerance, gentleness, simplicity and selflessness, Buddhism had a tremendous civilizing effect on Southeast Asia. Buddhism's very qualities, however, contain the kernels of its weaknesses. Its contemplative passivity may seem engaging. But its charming detachment from the turmoil of daily life has, at the same time, tended to make it largely a monastic exercise. There is little hope for the layman, unable to follow every detail of the way of righteousness, to fulfill the requirements for reaching nirvana. In its attractive tolerance, Buddhism also lays itself open to contamination.

Throughout Burma, Thailand and the other Buddhist lands of Southeast Asia, many monks heretically cast horoscopes, read palms and tell fortunes. A Burmese peasant would not even consider plowing a field until the abbot of his local temple has consulted astrological tables to calculate the propitious day to begin. Like western businessmen seeing their lawyers, sophisticated Bangkok merchants visit soothsayers for counsel before consummating important deals. Thailand's leaders are advised by astrologers and fortune-tellers who, in effect, share in handling affairs of state. A devout Buddhist, the Laotian Prince Boun Oum Na Champassak wears a *luk krok*—an amulet supposedly made from a human fetus—which is said to be capable of rendering him invisible.

MANY of these apparent superstitions are syncretic mixtures of different religions. Hindu rites persist in Buddhist and Moslem countries. A Thai village, for example, may have its *Nai Phram,* or Brahman, a layman possessed of great mystical lore. He can chant at the bedside of the sick or place consecrated threads around a house to ward off omens. Similar Hindu relics survive among the Moslems of Malaya, where children wear topknots of hair and an infant at birth is sung a verse from the Hindu hymnal, the Rig-Veda, to wish him long life and happiness. In the Philippines, oriental ancestor worship mingles with Roman Catholicism. On All Saints' Day, for instance, whole families flock to the cemeteries to light joss sticks and candles on the graves of the departed.

Medicine men of every shade and stamp thrive in Southeast Asian lands. In Burma, there is the *weik-za,* who concocts rejuvenating powders, and in Malaya the *pawang* is reputed to do anything from provoking rain to curing arthritis. There are thousands of *dukuns* in Indonesia, and one of their specialities is a brew called *djamu,* made from barks, leaves, herbs and roots and particularly favored by women after pregnancy. Although he is a Moslem, Indonesia's General Suharto is reported to lean on two different *gurus,* or native thaumaturgists. Former President Sukarno is known to have prayed to his *kris,* the ceremonial Malay dagger that symbolizes vitality and strength.

IT has often been asserted that the peoples of Southeast Asia, whatever their religions, are fundamentally animists. In Thailand and Laos, the ubiquitous spirits are called *phis,* and they are the objects of deep respect. Most *phis* are the ghosts of the dead, or they are spirits that reside in trees, brooks, mountains, stones and plants. Almost every Thai and Laotian home has its little garden shrine containing an offering of rice or fruit to propitiate these invisible elves. The *nats* of Burma are more clearly divided into three groups: nature spirits, ancestral phantoms or deities that may have descended from age-old Hindu mythology. The center of the *nat* cult in Burma is Mount Popa, southwest of Mandalay, and of the 37 spirits belonging to this formal pantheon, several are historical figures. A couple of lesser *nats* are even Moslems, and their Buddhist followers dutifully abstain from eating pork.

No Southeast Asian would consciously anger a spirit, but the Burmese are especially generous to their *nats.* Former Prime Minister U Nu, although an internationally prominent Buddhist, always laid out a *bali nat sar,* or offering of food, for the spirits when he traveled around the country, and before his government was toppled in 1962 he was planning to build two shrines for them, at a cost of $20,000 each. A case of far more fervent feeling toward a *nat* was revealed in September 1961, when a Rangoon newspaper reported that a young man named Maung Kyi Aye, aged 21, was betrothed to marry Min Mahagiri, the guardian spirit of his parents' household. "As the wedding is to be between a *nat* and a mere human being," commented the newspaper, "local interest has been greatly stimulated."

Members of the Cao Dai sect, which combines elements of Buddhism, Christianity and Taoism, worship in their ornate Vietnam oratory.

A Complex Mixture of Many Religions

Through the centuries, the religious beliefs in Southeast Asia have combined and cross-fertilized until the area is a jungle of doctrinal exotica. Buddhism in some regions has been mixed with Hinduism. Islam, coming later, absorbed many of the elements of these earlier faiths. Even Christianity accommodated itself to lingering primitive animism. But perhaps in no other part of the world is everyday life more permeated by religious custom and observance.

IMPORTED CREEDS, Islam and Christianity

were brought to Southeast Asia by traders, merchants, colonists and missionaries

INDONESIAN MOSLEMS chat in the street *(opposite)* near their small, unadorned mosque. Their black velvet hats are traditional with the islands' Mohammedan majority.

PHILIPPINE CATHOLICS attend Mass in one of the country's many churches. Brought by the Spanish, Roman Catholicism claims about two thirds of the islands' people.

HINDUISM, first of the Indian religions to flood eastward, still has many faithful followers

PILGRIMS throng the steep stairway *(opposite)* leading to the Batu caves near Kuala Lumpur in Malaysia. Many of Malaysia's Hindus are of Indian origin or ancestry and practice extreme forms of Hindu piety, including self-torture. Some who come to Batu seek absolution by piercing their skin with hundreds of nails, spikes and pins.

PRAYERS are offered a carved elephant by a young Balinese woman on the animal's "birthday" *(right)*. On Bali, Hinduism long ago became blended with a primitive worship of good and evil spirits. Unlike other Indonesians, the Balinese remained loyal to their strange, mixed Hinduism when Mohammedanism came to the islands.

BUDDHISM lends life in Vietnam, Cambodia, Thailand, Burma and Laos an intensely spiritual tone

MEDITATING MONKS in Bangkok, Thailand, a great center of Buddhist worship *(above)*, hold the sacred cord which is passed among them during a "merit-working" ceremony. It unites the worshipers in the blessing of the sacred text.

ELABORATE SETTING frames a great Buddha in Bangkok's Wat Bovornives monastery *(opposite)* where monks gather to pray. The Buddha's right hand points downward, symbolizing his appeal to the earth to bear witness to his virtue.

DEVOUT GATHERING in Rangoon, presided over by an ancient Buddhist patriarch, celebrates the 2,500th anniversary of Buddha's birth. Participants meet in a facsimile of the cave where the first Buddhist Synod occurred in 483 B.C.

FANTASTIC PAGODA, the massive Shwe Dagon, which stands on a hillside in Rangoon, Burma, gleams with tons of gold leaf before a group of meditating monks. Pious laymen often buy the gold leaf and clamber up the pagoda to apply it themselves. This is an act of merit for the believer and helps bring him closer to the timeless,

peaceful realm of nirvana, the ultimate goal of the Buddhist. Merit is also accumulated by scrubbing the terrace before the pagoda, and even high officials of the Burmese government can sometimes be observed washing it down with brooms. The main pagoda *(background)* is 326 feet high and is surrounded by 64 small, spired shrines.

CHINESE FESTIVAL is celebrated with burning joss sticks and special food by a group of overseas Chinese in Malacca. Some Chinese families have been in Malaysia for centuries, but they still observe their ancient customs.

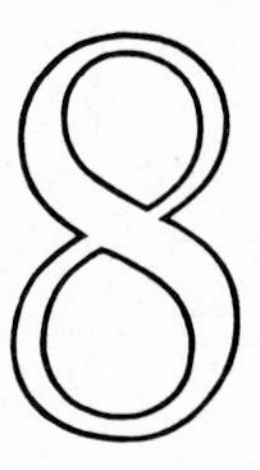

The Alien Sojourners

IN faraway Philippine villages they tend their tiny *sari-sari* shops by the light of kerosene lamps that flicker late into the night; in Bangkok's "thieves' market" they cautiously peddle rare Siamese antiques. They are moneylenders in Java, bankers in Saigon, smugglers in Borneo and rice merchants in Cambodia. In Malaysia, some are distinguished industrialists; others are Communist terrorists, lurking in the northern jungles. They are rugged coolies on Singapore's docks; and not many blocks away, at the city's luxurious Chinese restaurants, they arrive in Cadillacs and Daimlers to dine on sharks' fins and suckling pig. Dissimilar as they seem, all these people are tied together by a strong, common bond—they are Chinese. There are an estimated 14.5 million overseas Chinese in Southeast Asia, and nowhere in the world is an alien community so vital an economic force—and of such potential political importance.

They call themselves *hua-chiao,* sojourning Chinese, and the term is significant. They are colonists who are not quite settlers, residents who often cannot or will not become citizens of the lands they inhabit. They are always conscious that they are heirs to the 4,000 years of the history and the traditions of China, the "middle kingdom" which regarded itself as the civilized center of a world peopled by barbarians. Paradoxically, they have lived abroad for generations, jealously guarding their customs, thriving by extraordinary energy and enterprise, suffering the inevitable persecution of prosperous outcasts.

In South Vietnam, the overseas Chinese have been under pressure to change their names and abandon their language. In Cambodia, they are barred from 18 specific professions—among them barbering, pawnbroking and, strangely enough, espionage. Suspected of opium dealing or burning their stores for insurance, they have been summarily shot in Thailand. Efforts have been made to expel them from the Philippines and Indonesia, where ex-President Sukarno has claimed they "utilize the people's difficulties to get as much profit as possible."

But discrimination has not discouraged the overseas Chinese. On the contrary, it has strengthened their defensive clannishness and stimulated their drive toward success. They constitute less than 2 per cent of the Philippine population but, among other things, control two thirds of the country's lucrative copra export trade. A mere 8 per cent of South Vietnam's people, they are essential middlemen in the trading of tea, coffee, rice, kapok and rubber. In Malaysia, where they comprise more than 40 per cent of the population, they operate most of the trucking and bus companies, hold large rubber and tin interests, and receive about 60 per cent of the national income. Numbering roughly 10 per cent of Thailand's population, they run 90 per cent of retail business and dominate the rice and export timber trades. In 1914, Thailand's Oxford-educated King Vajiradvudh railed against the overseas Chinese as "the Jews of the Orient," and that expression is still repeated.

Such criticism is charged with emotion and envy. In most countries of the area, the Chinese have reaped their rewards by the sort of determination and hard work that is foreign to many of Southeast Asia's indigenous peoples. The Indonesian cabdriver in Djakarta, for example, cheerfully goes home when he has earned 100 *rupiahs;* a Chinese family will work from dawn until dusk constructing rattan furniture, then move tables and chairs out in front of their shop and operate a restaurant until midnight. They carefully husband their capital and make shrewd investments, and the annals of the *hua-chiao* are filled with true Horatio Alger stories. An obscure Malaccan schoolteacher named Tan Cheng-lock tried his hand at rubber planting in 1908 and became the possessor of a fortune whose size he could not estimate and a knight of the British Empire. Lim Tsing-chong went to Burma at the turn of the century as a coolie, graduated to street hawking, put his money in rubber and tin, and died a multimillionaire. Early in the 1900s, Tan Kah-kee settled in Singapore. After twenty years he had built up an empire of plantations, newspapers and shipping and trucking lines and had given away $10 million founding educational institutions.

Except in one or two countries, where they have made long-term investments in factories and rubber estates, most overseas Chinese gamble for a quick return on their money. They bid for rice harvests and speculate in real estate, keeping their cash as liquid as possible, and smuggling upward of $100 million per year out of their lands of residence to Hong Kong, where the British colonial government

CHINESE IN SOUTHEAST ASIA

	Total Population	Chinese
Burma	25,246,000	375,000
Thailand	31,508,000	3,726,000
Laos	2,635,000	40,000
Cambodia	6,250,000	350,000
North Vietnam	19,000,000	140,000
South Vietnam	16,124,000	1,450,000
West Malaysia	8,298,000	3,000,000
Sarawak	862,000	270,000
Sabah	551,000	124,000
Singapore	1,914,000	1,440,000
Brunei	104,000	27,500
Indonesia	104,500,000	3,100,000
Philippines	33,477,000	400,000
Totals	250,469,000	14,442,500

fosters discreet economic freedom. This flight capital has transformed Hong Kong into a fabulous boom town with exciting industries and giddy land prices. It has, however, deprived Southeast Asia's economies of money much needed for investment. But the overseas Chinese argue that their status is too uncertain to permit them the luxury of long-range risks. As a *hua-chiao* merchant in Bangkok puts it, "I have seen too much war and persecution in my lifetime to have much faith in security."

THE same sort of nervous commercial drive has motivated the overseas Chinese as far back as history recalls. There is evidence that seafaring Chinese traders followed the coast of southern China down to the shores of present-day Vietnam as early as 300 B.C. By the 12th and 13th Centuries, Chinese commerce in Southeast Asia was so well organized that merchants had a shipping guide, the *Record of Foreign Nations,* to aid their operations. Four-masted junks carried porcelain, damasks, brocades and satins, musk and rhubarb to the region they called *Nanyang,* the "Southern Ocean," and returned with spices, coral, birds' nests, herbs and other merchandise. Encouraged by the Sung Dynasty emperors, *Nanyang* trade yielded revenues that are said to have covered a large percentage of Chinese government expenses at home.

Traders' and sailors' tales conjured up heady visions of wealth abroad, and thousands of Chinese merchants set forth to Siam, Brunei, Malacca, Sumatra and the Philippines to seek their fortune. At the turn of the 17th Century, a Chinese commercial expert published *Of the Eastern and Western Seas,* a manual pinpointing Chinese trading posts in Southeast Asia, and they were everywhere. When Europeans entered the area, they found, as the English adventurer Sir Thomas Herbert wrote in 1634, that every major seaport was filled with the "infinitely industrious Chyneses."

The European powers were initially hesitant and ambiguous in their attitude toward the Chinese. Impressed by Chinese skill, they were worried by the possibility of Chinese rivalry, and serious tensions developed. In Manila, for example, the Spanish tried to confine the Chinese to certain quarters of the town, and revolts broke out in which more than 50,000 Chinese perished during the 17th Century. Similarly fearful of competition, the Dutch murdered thousands of Chinese in Java. But before long, the colonial nations and the overseas Chinese recognized that they were more complementary than competitive. The one supplied the technology and power, the other shrewdness and hard work; between them they could amass the mighty riches of the Indies.

The alliance of European strength with *hua-chiao* ingenuity and labor became a pattern throughout Southeast Asia. The Chinese spread as the Dutch extended their control over the Indonesian archipelago and followed the British and the French into the interiors of Burma and Indochina. When the British began to tap the resources of Malaya in the 19th Century, they cast about for more diligent workers than the native Malays. Southern China at the time was a distressed, overcrowded region ravaged by floods and rebellions. Impoverished peasants were willing to go anywhere, and labor brokers organized the "pig trade," packing people into flimsy junks and shipping them off to Southeast Asia like African slaves. Chinese went to work in tin mines and on pepper estates, and when rubber cultivation was introduced into Malaya, many labored on the new plantations. Thousands died in the mines and fields and in shipwrecks, and hundreds of thousands spent their lives in bleak poverty. But astonishing numbers learned new techniques with bewildering speed.

INNATE gamblers, the overseas Chinese rapidly built up their interests in mining and agriculture, shopkeeping and transportation, and they very soon came to see the value of western economic institutions. They began to get into financing and banking, import-export firms, light industry and the management of large estates. Clever and adaptable, they fast realized that western steamships and railroads would destroy the monopoly of coastal shipping commanded by their junks. They switched to trucking, and today the overseas Chinese largely dominate road transportation throughout Southeast Asia. Nor were they squeamish about penetrating the most primitive jungle areas. They probed into backward villages to sell manufactured goods to peasants, to collect harvests for market, to mortgage crops and, in some places, to become creditors of entire rural populations. Contrary to popular myth they were often lenient moneylenders.

CHINESE fortunes did not always grow out of hard work. Living on the margins of society, the *hua-chiao* felt no great compulsion to function with strict legality. They made money in smuggling and the black market, and such activities were facilitated by the complicated Chinese family nexus spread throughout Southeast Asia. It is possible, for example, to pay $100 to a money-changer in Hong Kong and three days later pick up the equivalent in Burmese *kyats* or Indonesian *rupiahs* from his cousin in Rangoon or Djakarta—at the black market rate. Overseas Chinese are especially adept at wining and bribing local officials, and as one *hua-chiao* businessman has explained it: "We like two kinds of government: one that is honest and orderly so you know what is coming, and the other that is frankly corrupt but keeps its word in its illegal dealings."

In their own defense, the Chinese point out that impracticable government regulations and red tape in many of Southeast Asia's countries make honest business impossible. They claim that inefficient Indonesian efforts to control the rubber trade render it far more simple to smuggle rubber out of Sumatra than to export it legally. In addition, they explain that it is impossible to honor the legal rate of the Indonesian *rupiah* when the currency is virtually worthless.

The Chinese also complain that they are harassed by discriminatory practices. To become a Cambodian citizen, for example, a candidate must make a number of pay-offs to expedite his application. Complications of this sort are similar in other Southeast Asian countries, and therefore few *hua-chiao* become naturalized. In the Philippines, Vietnam, Thailand and Burma, however, a good many have become assimilated through intermarriage, and it is difficult to estimate how many people in these countries have Chinese blood. The Philippine national heroes José Rizal and Emilio Aguinaldo were part Chinese, as was the late mayor of Manila, Arsenio Lacson, whose name was a corruption of English and Fukienese, meaning "sixth son." Burma's prime minister, General Ne Win, has Chinese antecedents, as do many of Thailand's leading officials, among them Foreign Minister Thanat Khoman.

Most overseas Chinese, however, are profoundly attached to their special identity, and wherever the *hua-chiao* may be, racial mystique starts from infancy. Language is an essential element in national solidarity, and in Chinese schools throughout Southeast Asia, children are told that Chinese is the greatest language in the world, with the greatest number of characters, spoken by the greatest number of people. From that it is only a simple step to the conclusion that China is the greatest nation in the world, and millions of school children are enjoined to repeat the slogan: *"Wo shih Chung Kuo jen. Wo chu tsai Nanyang. Wo ai Chung Kuo."* (I am Chinese. I live in the Southern Ocean. I love China.)

STARTING with the family, the basic unit, overseas Chinese have a complex assortment of social ties. They are enrolled in different regional organizations—The Swatow Association or The Fukien Residents Benevolent Brotherhood—and they may belong to a staggering list of other clubs and fraternities, trade unions, protective groups or convivial federations. In many areas there are notorious secret societies, such as the Triad.

Originally a quasi-religious fraternity which developed in south China in the 17th Century, the Triad—or trinity of heaven, earth and man—was dedicated to overturning the alien Manchus and restoring the Ming Dynasty. Its initial purpose was eventually forgotten, and the Triad spawned a baffling variety of lesser branches and imitations. Some were political, like Dr. Sun Yat-sen's Tung Meng Hui, or Sworn Brothers' Society, a forerunner of the Kuomintang, the group that engineered the Chinese Revolution of 1911 and made Sun Yat-sen China's first president. Other organizations with names like the Heaven and Earth Society or the Prosperity and Loyalty Society degenerated into little more than outlaw gangs, terrorizing poor Chinese tin miners and coolies. Secret societies are still active in Singapore and Malaya, where their favorite pastime is kidnaping Chinese millionaires, sometimes sending the victim's ear pinned to the first ransom note.

IN their various countries of residence today, the overseas Chinese are understandably a thorny problem, and Southeast Asian governments would like to get rid of them. But the *hua-chiao* are indispensable to the maintenance of trade and commerce, and their economic importance is privately recognized by national leaders. In the Philippines, politicians regularly inveigh against the "alien" scapegoat, but it is no secret that many depend on Chinese businessmen for campaign contributions. Overseas Chinese are constantly threatened in Thailand, yet several prominent Bangkok officials engage in slightly illicit commercial dealings through local Chinese intermediaries. Not long ago, in fact, a distinguished Thai minister was much embarrassed to discover that his private Chinese entrepreneur was also a Communist agent. In 1959, when Indonesia's President Sukarno sternly ordered Chinese traders out of the villages into the cities, he found that there was nobody to handle rural commerce. He was also shocked when Red China came to the aid of its compatriots abroad. The Indonesian foreign minister was summoned to Peking where, as one diplomat put it, he was treated "like an errant schoolboy."

The rulers of both Nationalist and Communist China have vacillated in their attitudes toward the overseas Chinese. Anxious to win friends, the Formosa government has tended to sacrifice the interests of the *hua-chiao* for the sake of possible good relations with Southeast Asian states. Red China has had the power to play it both ways. In the first flush of triumph after conquering the mainland, the Communists championed the overseas Chinese. They were allotted 30 seats in the National People's Congress in Peking, saluted as "the endeared people of the Chinese nation" and assured that their "proper rights and interests are now protected by their country."

The overseas Chinese proudly swung to the support of the new regime. Thousands of Chinese students flocked back to the mainland, Chinese millionaires endowed schools and hospitals in China, and millions of dollars in remittances poured back to *hua-chiao* relatives in the homeland. As a wealthy Singapore Chinese explained to the American reporter Robert Elegant: "Don't you see? They've made China strong and respected. Anyone who can do that deserves all our help. We must serve the Communists, even if we don't like them."

SOON afterward, however, a period of disenchantment set in. Red China decided that the Southeast Asian states were momentarily more important than the overseas Chinese, and Red China's Premier Chou En-lai, wooing the Afro-Asian bloc at the Bandung Conference in Indonesia in 1955, urged that Chinese abroad "be loyal to the countries they live in." This shift in strategy was followed by a growing disillusionment among the overseas Chinese with the Communists. Students returning from Red China reported on the hardships of life under Communism. Relatives saw little of the money remitted to them, and there were even more gruesome tales of ancestral graves demolished and people corralled into communes.

It rapidly occurred to the Communists that their new policy was not winning many friends among the countries of Southeast Asia, and it was losing them the support of the overseas Chinese. Again the line changed. Peking's propagandists stoutly defended the oppressed Chinese traders in Indonesia, and Red China's stock again rose among the *hua-chiao*. Appalled as they might be by conditions in China, many overseas Chinese believe that they have a protector, and such achievements by the Peking regime as the development of nuclear weapons have served to stir the national pride of even avowed anti-communist overseas Chinese.

If many overseas Chinese think that they can rely on Peking, Red China is also persuaded that the *hua-chiao* are a useful fifth column. Communist agents have infiltrated into schools and trade unions and in countries that recognize the Peking regime, they operate overtly.

In the old days, the Chinese in Burma lived their esoteric social lives within a traditional framework of clan associations and secret societies. But when the Chinese People's Republic opened its embassy in Rangoon in 1949, Peking's emissaries created a new context for the local Chinese. The embassy, with its red-and-gold lacquer gates, became the center of cultural and social activities, offering a swimming pool and other amenities for *hua-chiao* children. With the deterioration of relations between Burma and Peking in 1967, however, the Chinese Embassy in Rangoon assumed a new function: in effect, it turned into a kind of fortified headquarters in which local Chinese, surrounded by a hostile population, could seek solace and protection.

COMMUNIST influence in Southeast Asia is perhaps best exerted in the domain where the overseas Chinese are most sensitive—business. An important instrument for Peking's extension of influence are communist-controlled banks. If a local Chinese merchant is sympathetic, cooperative and possessed of the proper political outlook, he can get unlimited credit, often without collateral. All he need do is show the signatures of two approved witnesses and promise to send his children to a communist school. To make matters look tidy, the banks go through the motions of collecting interest on their loans. But a debtor who behaves correctly has no cause for concern. His defaulting can be overlooked, and in time the whole transaction may be forgotten.

An overseas Chinese who stubbornly chooses to resist such generosity may find himself in difficulties. One morning, as he opens his shop, he may be surprised to find a competitor moving in next door or across the street. The rival's shop will be neat and clean and stocked with miraculous bargains—mechanical toys, canned goods or sewing machines bearing the stamp "Made in China." And even if his business tends to be chronically bad, the competitor can hold out with remarkable endurance, as if he were being subsidized by some outside source —which, of course, he is.

OUTWARDLY, the allegiances of the overseas Chinese constitute an enigma. In countries that recognize the Chinese Nationalists—the Philippines, South Vietnam and Thailand—*hua-chiao* merchants display portraits of Chiang Kai-shek in their shops. In Burma, Cambodia and Indonesia, which recognize Red China, stores show pictures of Mao Tse-tung. And in Malaysia, which recognizes neither China, the hero is Sun Yat-sen. Each stance can be called patriotism, and patriotism, the merchant is sure to explain, "is good for business."

This kind of diplomatic demonstration displays nothing so much as the fact that the Chinese abroad is primarily loyal to himself. And from that self-centered posture, he will swing to whichever side benefits him more. Even in the avowed anti-Communist states of Southeast Asia, his secret sympathies have leaned toward Red China. He is sentimentally attached to the motherland, and he respects whichever power controls it. The only alternative to this situation may be assimilation. But neither the governments of the region nor the *hua-chiao* themselves are approaching that solution, and for years to come the overseas Chinese are likely to remain a separate, doubtful state within the states of Southeast Asia.

Chinese tellers tally stacks of bills and coins in a British-owned bank in Singapore, long the banking center of the Malay Peninsula.

Diligent Outsiders in Unfriendly Lands

More than 14 million Chinese live in Southeast Asia. Many were brought in as coolies, and in some countries they are now persecuted by the natives. Even so, they have been remarkably successful. Fiercely proud of their Chinese heritage, they have a diligence and a financial acumen that make them essential to the economic growth of the nations they inhabit. And in Singapore, where they form 75 per cent of the population, they hold the reins of government.

CULTURAL TIES remain strong among overseas Chinese as they seek to preserve their language and identity

GIGANTIC POOL belonging to a Chinese swimming club in Singapore gets scrubbed by a solitary workman. Membership in the club is open only to Chinese, and they have a number of other exclusive organizations in Singapore.

HISTORICAL OPERA, sung by actors in Chinese costume *(left)*, is presented by a road company at a theater in Bangkok, Thailand. The operas, popular with the Chinese community, tell stories drawn from Chinese history and legend.

CHINESE CLASSROOM in Thailand has posters printed in both the Chinese and Thai languages urging the students to keep the school clean and to mind their manners. Chinese education persists in Thailand despite opposition.

WORSHIPING WOMEN emerge from the temple of Sam Po Kong in Semarang, Java. Sam Po Kong is the spirit of a 15th Century Chinese admiral who explored Southeast Asia and is believed to protect the Chinese in foreign lands.

ENTERPRISE aided by cooperation among themselves has helped the Chinese thrive despite local prejudices

FRIENDLY MEETING of Chinese leaders in Manila is addressed by Yu Khe Thai, a highly successful banker and philanthropist. The Chinese once dominated Philippine commerce but now suffer from discriminatory practices.

CIVIC LEADER in Thailand, the late Yun Chu-ting poses in the home he built with a fortune gained manufacturing ice. He was a citizen of Thailand but continued to be active in a number of overseas Chinese associations.

PRIME MINISTER of Singapore, Lee Kuan Yew *(below)* visits a housing project. Son of a Chinese shipping magnate, Lee was a brilliant law student at Cambridge, England, then returned to Singapore a staunch anti-colonial.

As dusk settles over jungle-clad hills which hide fast-striking squads of Communist guerrillas, two sentries of the Royal Laotian Army

guard an outpost near Samneua, a small village in northern Laos.

9

An Active, Elusive Enemy

MONSOON heat drugged the morning air as two South Vietnamese army battalions swiftly encircled a small island in the mangrove swamps of the Mekong River delta south of Saigon. At a signal they attacked, plunging deep into the dense marshes, hacking through the tangled foliage. Hours later they retired, bombarded the area with artillery fire and air strikes, and attacked again. For three days and nights the assaults continued. Finally the weary troops withdrew, ravaged by mosquitoes and leeches. They had not seen their enemy—a company of Communist guerrillas—and their commanding colonel remarked sadly, "We are too exhausted to carry on."

Such frustrating operations typify the nagging, dirty war in Vietnam, which grew from a small Communist insurgency into a major conflict engaging half a million American troops and many billions of U.S. dollars. It is a conflict, too, that soon became an international issue, involving Red China and the Soviet Union as well as the United States and its Asian allies. Yet it is a struggle that the Communists, despite their inferiority in materiel, have managed to prolong because of their skill in guerrilla tactics and their experience in what is essentially political warfare.

In the era of colonialism, the Communists purported to be nationalists. During the more recent days of independence they have gone a step further, propagating plans for social and economic action. And their formula for revolution is often attractive, especially to Southeast Asia's youth, because it challenges apathetic, confused or corrupt governments which are often intent on preserving a *status quo* of power and privilege. Although Red China is in turmoil, the mystique of Marxism still sways many Asians, as it has for generations.

COMMUNISM began to bud in Asia in the early decades of the 20th Century. Lenin contended that the capitalist nations of Europe had exported their surplus capital to backward countries where land was cheap, raw materials plentiful, wages low and profits high. Therefore, he concluded, capitalism was at the root of colonialism. This debatable theory captivated many young intellectuals in the Orient. It was a western notion to which they could subscribe without appearing "pro-colonial," and many automatically equated communism and nationalism. Quick to realize the appeal of this logic, the Soviet Communists started preparing to penetrate Asia soon after the Russian Revolution. As early as September 1920, a congress of "Peoples of the East" was held in the Soviet Union, and at about the same time schools for Asian revolutionaries and propagandists were opened in Moscow and elsewhere.

Like characters out of a Graham Greene suspense novel, secret Communist agents popped up everywhere in the Far East during the 1920s. In Java, the Dutch engineer Hendrik Sneevliet, alias Maring, transferred his Marxist Social-Democratic Association to Communist control. An Indonesian Comintern operative named Tan Malaka, disguised as a musician, turned up in Manila to help found the Philippine Communist party. In 1925 Ho Chi Minh, already a veteran in the Communist apparatus, arrived in Canton, ostensibly to serve as a translator for the Soviet consulate, in reality to recruit Vietnamese refugees in south China into an Association of Vietnamese Revolutionary Youth.

This and other young Communist movements in Southeast Asia suffered from several handicaps. They were sometimes zealous beyond their means, and they exposed themselves wildly to inevitable repressions. At their first congress, the Philippine Communists announced their intention to "seize control . . . and establish a government like that of the Soviets," and they were promptly outlawed. Even more ambitious, the Indonesian Communists tried to stage a full-scale coup d'état in 1927, and they were easily destroyed by the Dutch. In Singapore and Malaya, the South Seas Communist party launched a series of strikes, and its leaders were arrested by the British police. Often these abortive uprisings were the result of Soviet policy—for, as would be demonstrated in later decades, the Kremlin considered foreign Communists expendable.

AFTER such disasters, it was remarkable that Communist movements in Southeast Asia ever survived at all. During the 1930s they had little to do with the growth of nationalism, and not until the Japanese occupation did some of the groups rise to action. In Malaya, Vietnam and the Philippines they organized guerrilla forces, but these were frequently designed to eliminate their political opponents rather than the enemy. In the Philippines during World War II, for example, the Hukbong Bayan Laban Sa Hapon, or People's Anti-Japanese Resistance Army—known as the Huks—killed an estimated 5,000 Japanese and liquidated some 20,000 of its Filipino rivals.

In the years immediately after the war, the Communists were confused and unsettled. Late in 1947, however, the first public hint of a new revolutionary policy emerged. At a Warsaw meeting of the Cominform—the newly formed organization of international Communist parties—the Soviet delegate Andrei Zhdanov suggested that "the chief danger to the working class at the present juncture lies in underrating its own strength and overrating the strength of the enemy." This was a call to action, couched in subtle Communist jargon, and it was accompanied by a series of surreptitious comings and goings. Malayan Communists went to London to attend a meeting of British Communists; an important Indonesian Communist returned home from Moscow; and a significant Communist youth congress was held in Calcutta, at which Southeast Asia was described as "the central arena of the struggle for national liberation against imperialism." As the pattern of events to follow proved, 1948 was to be the year of revolution in the region.

ONE of the first fields for insurrection was the Philippines, which the Communists essayed as an area ripe for revolt. The Philippine government was corrupt and inept, and there were genuine social grievances among the country's peasants, almost half of whom were miserably impoverished tenant farmers. Veteran guerrillas of the war against the Japanese, the Huks were effective fighters. By the end of 1948 their uprising was gathering momentum, and within little more than a year they were threatening Manila.

It has perhaps never been wholly realized how close the Philippines came to falling to the Communists, and how the country was saved by a single man, Ramon Magsaysay. A former bus mechanic who had fought with the Americans against the Japanese and was later elected to the Philippine Congress, Magsaysay was appointed secretary of defense in 1950. Sincere, courageous and tough, Magsaysay grasped immediately that most of the Communist-led rank and file were rebelling against poverty and oppression, and he called his policy one of "All-Out Force and All-Out Friendship." He reorganized the Philippine army into mobile combat teams to pursue the fast-moving Huks, built up a broad intelligence network and protected terrorized villagers. And he paralleled military operations with psychological and economic efforts to win over the insurgents. "They want a house and land of their own," he said. "All right, they can stop fighting because I will give it to them. And if they are not satisfied with that, by golly, I have another big deal for them. I am going to set up a carpentry shop and let the Huks run it."

Elected president in 1953, Magsaysay worked vigorously to stamp out corruption. By 1957, when he tragically died in an airplane crash, Magsaysay had almost completely eradicated the Communist menace. However, no subsequent Philippine government has grappled with the core of the country's problems. Unemployment is widespread, corruption is common and the plight of the poor peasant has not been ameliorated. In this distress lie the seeds of potential trouble.

The Cominform's signal to rebel in 1948 also activated the Malayan Communists, who revived the same underground units they had created to battle the Japanese. But these insurgents faced a difficult task. They were mainly overseas Chinese easily distinguishable from the Malays; they were trying to function in a country poor in food; and the Malayan population, on whom British rule had rested lightly, was not an unhappy people thirsting for liberation. Nevertheless, the Communists were able to muster as many as 11,000 men during the height of their struggle, and they were actively aided by the Min Yuen, a "people's movement" of sympathizers who provided them with food, money, intelligence and recruits. It took British Commonwealth troops more than a decade to defeat the terrorists.

THE most dramatic and successful Communist operation in Southeast Asia was ignited in Vietnam even before Moscow issued its revolutionary directives, and out of it came the only Communist state and the strongest military power in Southeast Asia. Created in 1941 as a "national front" to fight the Japanese, the Vietnam Doc Lap Dong Minh Hoi, or

League for the Independence of Vietnam—better known as the Viet Minh—expanded after World War II. In the southern parts of the country the Communists gradually established their committees in rural areas. In the north they were able to purchase substantial supplies of weapons from the black marketeering Chinese Nationalists who were then occupying the region, and the Viet Minh was well prepared to fight the French when hostilities erupted at Haiphong in December 1946.

UNLIKE the other Communist movements of Southeast Asia, which mostly missed the nationalist boat, the Viet Minh did in fact become the principal force for nationalism in Vietnam. Under Ho Chi Minh and General Vo Nguyen Giap, a former schoolteacher, it also perfected an army that fought and defeated the French in eight years of war. Using the principles of guerrilla conflict formulated by Mao Tse-tung in China, the Viet Minh learned the arts of individual mobility, winning peasant support, capturing arms, avoiding cities and controlling rural areas. Assisted by the Chinese Communists, who provided arms, technical advice and asylum over the border, the Viet Minh was superior to the cream of France's professional soldiers because it knew how to fight in Vietnam. "We hold the towns, the road nets, the harbors and the airfields," wrote a frustrated French officer. "We hold everything, but the enemy is everywhere."

Unquestionably skillful at war, the Vietnamese Communists proved less proficient at peace. Assigned by the Geneva Conference of 1954 to the Vietnam territory north of the 17th parallel, the Communists tried to imitate the policies of Red China, with disappointing results. They concentrated on developing industry and made some progress. But they suffered serious setbacks in agriculture. They staged a brutal land reform program—unnecessary in a region in which two thirds of the farmers owned their property—and they further alienated peasants by enforcing a scheme for "producers' cooperatives." As in China itself, food production in North Vietnam has lagged badly. This shortcoming has been aggravated by a staggering birth rate of 3.5 per cent per year, which has raised the country's population to more than 16 million. To satisfy their need for rice, the Communists are looking to the south, traditionally Vietnam's source of food.

"To reunify the fatherland is the sacred and inviolable right of the Vietnamese people," say the propaganda broadcasts from Hanoi, North Vietnam's capital, and Communist guerrillas are on the move everywhere in South Vietnam. Many of them are veterans who remained in the swamplands of the Mekong River delta after the Indochina war; others are southerners who were sent north in 1955 for training and have been infiltrated back to their home areas through the uncontrolled regions of neighboring Laos and Cambodia. In December 1960 they founded a National Liberation Front of South Vietnam, and despite United States military intervention, the anti-Communist government in Saigon has been hard put to handle the insurrection. To a large extent, the Communists have capitalized on Saigon's shortcomings. Unlike Magsaysay, the government has been slow to recognize the need for military mobility or the kind of political appeals that stir the popular imagination. Thus the fight against the Communists in Vietnam turned out to be long and costly.

THE Vietnamese Communists were also effective in building an insurgent movement in Laos. Viet Minh instructors had trained Laotian nationalists as early as 1946, and in 1949 the Laotian Prince Souphanouvong—who had been educated in Hanoi and Paris, and was married to a Vietnamese—traveled to North Vietnam. An eternal rebel with pronounced leftist leanings, Souphanouvong was seeking help to liberate Laos from French rule. In a rudimentary jungle camp he met General Vo Nguyen Giap, the Viet Minh commander, who gave him advice on training insurgents. Not long after, the "Red Prince" formed his Communist-oriented organization, the Pathet

Lao, or Land of the Lao. In later years, when the Pathet Lao was actively fighting in Laos, its ranks were filled with Vietnamese Communist technicians skilled in communications, guerrilla warfare and the use of artillery. Now the strongest military and political figure in Laos, Souphanouvong owes his power to North Vietnam, and indirectly to the Chinese Communists.

BY the early 1950s, Communist strategy in the Orient was beginning to change. The Russians had developed nuclear weapons, and the Chinese Communists had consolidated their hold over mainland China. Because it possessed the most modern arms and dominated the vast Sino-Soviet land mass, the Kremlin felt invincible. Without entirely abandoning their subversive tactics, the Communists now expounded to the world a new line—"peaceful coexistence."

This new approach coincided with changing attitudes among Asians. The establishment of a Communist regime in China was interpreted throughout the Far East as an anticolonial, nationalist victory. In addition, the Viet Minh's tenacity against the French in Indochina and Chinese Communist successes against the United States in the Korean war damaged western prestige. Many of the young Southeast Asian states curiously forgot their local Communist insurgents—most of whom had failed anyway—and reached out for the Soviet olive branch.

Under Stalin's successors—first Malenkov and then Khrushchev—the Russians demonstrated their pacific policies. They agreed to an armistice in the Korean stalemate, and they ended the Indochina war on terms that, as it turned out, were disadvantageous to the North Vietnamese. Special efforts were made to woo the Asian neutralists—who not long before had been termed "imperialist stooges"—and in this endeavor Chinese Communist Premier Chou En-lai turned on all his well-known charm. In April 1954 he joined with Jawaharlal Nehru of India in affirming the famous Panch Shila, or Five Principles, which included a declaration of mutual respect for each other's territorial integrity and sovereignty and pledges of peaceful coexistence and economic cooperation. A year later, at the Indonesian town of Bandung, some 340 delegates from 29 Afro-Asian countries gathered for a conference, and again Chou suavely reiterated Red China's desire to reduce tension and extend its friendship through the Far East.

This kind of Communist courtship had an electric effect in many quarters. Indonesia's President Sukarno flew off to the Soviet Union, where he was accorded an honorary doctorate by Moscow University, the Order of Lenin and $100 million in economic aid. From there he went to Peking, where Mao Tse-tung publicly supported the Indonesian campaign to acquire West New Guinea from the Dutch and Sukarno backed Red China's claim to Formosa. Slightly less emotional, Cambodia's Prince Sihanouk also included Moscow and Peking in his travels, and Premier Chou En-lai visited Cambodia. Another prominent Southeast Asian to tour the Communist circuit was Prince Souvanna Phouma, then prime minister of Laos.

But the Communists were not able to sustain a unified policy of respectability in the Far East, for the Soviet bloc began to split through its own "inner contradictions." Anxious to avoid war, which might destroy his modern industrial state, Khrushchev pursued a moderate line, urging Communist collaboration with "bourgeois nationalists" in underdeveloped countries. Mao Tse-tung, however, advocated a more dynamic, revolutionary approach. To a large degree, the rift in the Moscow-Peking axis has been reflected in Southeast Asia.

AFTER years of feting Indonesia's President Sukarno, the Chinese turned against him in 1959, and Khrushchev rushed off to Indonesia to retrieve the situation, spending two weeks in the broiling sun and soothing the *Bung* with a loan of $250 million. Peking has supported the extremist Prince Souphanouvong in Laos, while the Russians have been more temperate in backing the neutralist Prince Souvanna Phouma. The Soviets, who have an embassy in Bangkok, maintain friendly relations with Thailand; the Chinese sponsor a "Free Thai" movement, headed by the former Thai Prime Minister Pridi Phanomyong from his exile in Canton. However, the pattern is far from consistent. The Chinese have continued to appease Cambodia's Prince Sihanouk, plying him with ceremonial visits and aid programs. And as a lever against India, with which they are having a border war, the Chinese Communists have been extremely cordial toward the Burmese. In 1961 they settled an old frontier dispute with Burma, sealing the agreement with a loan of $84 million for industrial projects.

Whether propagated by Moscow or Peking, communism has not followed a straight, easily definable path in Southeast Asia. In many ways, this zigzagging course of communism has reflected the seesawing rivalry between the Soviet Union and Red China for influence in the area. In Malaysia, with its large ethnic Chinese population, Peking pulls the strings of an unseen but considerable Communist underground. No longer overtly terroristic, the Communists have infiltrated Malaysian schools and trade unions, and they carry a certain weight among the workers of neighboring Singapore. While apparently weak in ideology, the Communist Huks seem to be making a comeback in the Philippines, where they have been described as a "Red Mafia." They are especially powerful in the provinces of Central Luzon, an area of extreme peasant poverty which has a long and bitter record of populist opposition to successive governments in Manila.

THE most dramatic change in Communist fortunes in Southeast Asia occurred in Indonesia. Claiming some 3 million members and more than 10 million sympathizers, the Indonesian Communist movement was the largest in any non-Communist country. In September 1965, possibly following Peking's advice, the Communists staged an uprising presumably calculated to undermine their foes in the Indonesian army. The attempted coup d'état failed, however, prompting the army to embark upon a large-scale counterattack that shattered the country's Communist organization. The army action, moreover, led to the downfall of President Sukarno, who had tried to shield the Communists. It also resulted in a sharp deterioration of Indonesia's relations with Red China, thus straining ties that used to be known as the "Peking-Djakarta axis."

THE war in Vietnam has played a significant role in exacerbating tension between the Soviet Union and Red China. There is little doubt that the dynamism behind the Communist thrust in Vietnam has been generated in Hanoi, the capital of North Vietnam. In different ways and to varying degrees, Hanoi has been dependent on both Moscow and Peking for military assistance and political support. But the Russians have accused the Chinese of obstructing their aid shipments, while the Chinese have charged Moscow with "helping U.S. imperialism" in seeking a negotiated settlement of the war. The North Vietnamese Communists have so far managed to maintain a balance between the rival donors, taking aid from both without offending either.

In their Southeast Asia operations, the Chinese Communists would seem to have the advantage of being Asians themselves. Moreover, they have argued with some success that because their revolution took place in a backward country, it is a model for underdeveloped regions. Working against Peking, however, is the fact that many Southeast Asian Communist movements are deeply nationalistic, and thus anxious to avoid any form of Chinese or other foreign domination. It is noteworthy, for example, that for all its reliance on China, North Vietnam still evokes its historic struggle against the Chinese as one of its main appeals for domestic unity. The real threat in the region, therefore, is internal. For as the only Southeast Asian leader to defeat the Communists, Philippine President Ramon Magsaysay, once noted, outside economic and military intervention can be fruitless as long as a country "continues to foster and tolerate conditions which offer fertile soil to communism."

Carrying what they can, refugees leave Ben Suc after the hamlet had been razed to flush out Vietcong guerrillas and their supplies.

A Tenacious and Tormented People

For the Vietnamese, both north and south, both city dweller and farmer, destruction and violent death have become common hazards. For more than a quarter of a century the complex political forces that encircle the globe have clashed in Vietnam. That the citizens of this war-torn country have managed somehow to exist amidst and despite the deadly concussion reverberating around them attests to the fierce tenacity with which these people cling to life.

A TOTAL COMMITMENT to reunify Vietnam has fused the North Vietnamese into a tough and resourceful nation at war

A WORK BRIGADE of North Vietnamese men and women digs an irrigation canal. With only baskets to carry dirt, it takes hundreds of workers to complete a job that might be done by a single bulldozer. Nevertheless, such methods are effective: A road or a bridge, bombed out one day, is often repaired and back in use the next.

DOCK HANDS hold a "self-criticism" session in a public park in Haiphong, discussing how best to expedite their work. Such singlemindedness and dedication to a national purpose, inspired by the country's leader Ho Chi Minh, has made Communist North Vietnam, with a population of only 19 million, into a formidable force.

AIRCRAFT SPOTTERS, members of North Vietnam's militia, man a tower in a field near Haiphong. Here, as elsewhere in North Vietnam, signs of war are noticeable. The wall behind the tower, once part of an estate, now encloses a factory, while the vines and corn in the foreground are reminiscent of World War II victory gardens.

AN AIR RAID ALERT in Hanoi sends residents into small, manhole-like sidewalk shelters. Hardened by their nation's long struggle to liberate itself from French rule, the North Vietnamese have shown remarkable ingenuity in facing the perils of war, in keeping the country's economy going and in supplying the needs of their army.

TRAPPED between Vietcong terror and the blunt force of American arms, a bewildered South Vietnamese people struggle to survive

OXEN STRAIN to pull a cart *(left)* carrying a farm family and its rice crop to market near Saigon, while behind them some medium tanks of the U.S. First Infantry Division move up.

A FAMILY CRIES, not in pain but at the simple wonder of finding each other still alive after their village was overrun by the Vietcong, then retaken by South Vietnamese Rangers.

VOLUNTEERS HELP firemen play water on the wreckage of an ordnance depot in Saigon, probably sabotaged by the Vietcong, who over the years have become masters of such tactics.

Adult students attending a class in Jogjakarta offered by the Indonesian labor ministry eagerly raise their hands to answer a question.

Efforts to combat illiteracy have made great strides in Indonesia.

10

A Search for Stability

"WE do not see in Southeast Asia the kind of stability we might have hoped for after the last fifteen years of serious attention and effort," the U.S. Secretary of State, Dean Rusk, said in 1962. Similar expressions of disappointment are made frequently—and often sadly—by Southeast Asians themselves. For as they examine the region around them, they observe a disjointed, sometimes squabbling assortment of countries, most of them troubled by inadequate economic expansion, fragile political institutions, acute social tensions and, in many places, the threat of Communist subversion. In varying degrees, Southeast Asian states cannot look toward the future without serious apprehensions.

In Southeast Asia, as in other underdeveloped areas of the world, this is a time of change. In their individual, often puzzling ways, these countries are trying to transform their traditional societies into modern, sophisticated nations. In contrast to the nation-states of Europe, which matured slowly over the centuries, the countries of Asia—like those of Africa—were abruptly set free to shift for themselves. They have groped and stumbled in their attempts to adjust to the contemporary age. That these young Southeast Asian states have not achieved a healthy measure of internal progress is perhaps less surprising than the fact that they have somehow managed simply to survive.

HAZARDOUS and painful as the process of domestic development has been, it has been aggravated by another, overwhelming external factor. The new Asian states, penetrated and influenced by outside ideologies, have been thrown prematurely into the international arena. They have been deluged by competing foreign officials, ideas and organizations, all prepared to pay a price in aid money to win their allegiance. Under President Sukarno, for example, Indonesia succumbed to the temptations of foreign aid enticements to the extent of plunging itself some $2.5 billion in debt. The primitive land of Laos, to cite another case, was disrupted economically by overdoses of financial aid that it had neither the experience nor the competence to absorb properly.

At the same time, foreign military intervention in some countries, such as South Vietnam, has complicated and hampered domestic political growth. There seems to be no doubt that, through a combination of internal instability and growing Communist pressure, the Saigon government was doomed in early 1965. It was saved by rapid American help, both in the form of ground troops and air attacks against North Vietnam. Its increasing reliance on the United States, however, stunted the Saigon regime's evolution to the point where it abdicated many of its most important functions to Americans—who were, paradoxically, often bewildered and frustrated in their efforts to manage an alien oriental country.

If the Westerner is puzzled by Asia, the Asian himself is also often baffled by his country and its dilemmas. In a frank mood, he may add a note of sincere disenchantment to his perplexity. A Burmese army officer recently confessed to an American professor: "We expected so much from independence, and many of us have been disappointed. Ruling ourselves is much tougher than we realized, but we would never admit it publicly even now."

This phenomenon is common in young, newly sovereign states. The fight for freedom was simple and straightforward, and its goal was clear. But the problems of independence—like the troubles of adolescence—are painful, and the objectives are uncertain. And unhappily, the problems are accentuated by a general feeling among Southeast Asia's leaders that solutions must be found speedily if their countries are to catch up with the modern world. Thus there seems to be not enough time or concentration given to slow, careful development.

Southeast Asia is by no means similar to China or India, both of them regions of grinding poverty, hungry peasants and festering sores. Yet all of the area's lands face the immediate challenge of generating economic momentum. Some states, such as North Vietnam, Singapore and Indonesia, suffer from mounting population problems. The Philippines, where the contrasts between rich and poor are shockingly sharp, confronts potential social outbursts. Such rancor may take a racial form, as in Malaysia, where the wealth of urban Chinese clashes with the backwardness of rural Malays. Everywhere in Southeast Asia, there is an impending "revolution of expectations" from peoples faintly beginning to desire something more than shelter and clothing. Moreover, as producers of raw materials, Southeast Asian countries have come to recognize the dangers of dependence on whimsical world markets.

DIAGNOSING ills and outlining objectives are easier than prescribing policies. Southeast Asian countries have toyed with a catalogue of eclectic economic theories, schemes and nostrums. Many of these ideas were shaped by socialism, for comprehensible motives. Several leaders reasoned that their economic tasks were so enormous that only government could cope with them. They were also inclined, from their experiences as crusading nationalists, to associate capitalism with colonialism. By similar logic, some felt that the state could replace foreign ownership that was, they argued, a remnant of imperialism. "After all," runs a common theme in the area, "what good is political freedom without economic independence?"

ALTHOUGH private foreign investment is often suspect, foreign government aid has been considered generally desirable. Laos had depended almost entirely upon American assistance, and Indonesia has received extensive loans from both the United States and the Soviet Union. Cambodia accepts all offers from any nation, and a few years ago a writer in the London *Economist* remarked: "Theoretically, it will soon be possible for a lucky Cambodian pedestrian, who has been knocked down by a Polish steam locomotive, travelling to a port constructed by the French on a railway line built by the Chinese, to be rushed in an East German ambulance, driven by a Japanese-trained chauffeur and fuelled by American petrol, along a highway built by the Americans, to a modern hospital erected by the Russians and staffed by nurses using Czech equipment."

A remarkable paradox in the years since World War II has been the return of the Japanese to Southeast Asia. Under postwar reparations agreements and private business arrangements, Japanese salesmen, engineers, doctors and other technicians have again invaded the region—this time peacefully. Except in the Philippines, where wartime bitterness lingers on, Southeast Asian countries have welcomed the Japanese. The Japanese helped to build a hydroelectric project in Burma, and they are constructing a steel mill and other factories in Malaysia. Japanese economic assistance, including government aid, war reparations and private investment in Southeast Asia, has totaled more than two billion dollars. Ironically, it has often been suggested that the Japanese, who combine efficiency with Asian standards of living, might serve as a funnel for western aid into the non-communist Orient.

Dependence on foreign help does not mean that Southeast Asian states necessarily listen to foreign advice. Some of the countries, lacking experienced personnel and sufficient capital, have disregarded caution and embarked upon grandiose schemes that were doomed to failure from the outset. In January 1961, for example, Indonesia initiated its extravagant Eight-Year Plan to construct more than 350 major projects at a cost of $5.3 billion. At the end of the first year hardly anything had been accomplished. In the Philippines, mismanagement and corruption have frequently rendered aid funds ineffective, thereby disappointing both the donor and the recipient.

IF government guidance has proved unsuccessful in some areas, greater state economic participation could have helped in other places, especially in ameliorating rural conditions. Free enterprise stimulated a myriad of factories in Manila's suburbs, but there was little concern for the countryside, and the Philippine peasant's rice yield is one of the world's lowest. Alone in the region, Malaysia seems to have struck a sensible, progressive balance between private industrial investment and public development of its agricultural areas.

Indeed, no state in Southeast Asia has been so successful economically as Malaysia. Accepting virtually no foreign aid, Malaysia has shrewdly exploited its rich rubber plantations and tin deposits to build up substantial currency reserves. Using this money, the government recently launched a five-year rural development program aimed at opening up some 250,000 acres of arable land on which poor farm families can be resettled.

Out of Malaysia also came the original idea for regional cooperation in Southeast Asia. In 1958, Malaysia's prime minister, Prince Abdul Rahman, conceived the notion of an organization to strengthen economic and cultural ties among the countries of the area. In 1961 Malaysia, Thailand and the Philippines overcame their suspicions of one another enough to form a group which, in 1967, was joined by

Indonesia and Singapore and called the Association of Southeast Asian Nations (ASEAN). It remains to be seen, however, if the five nations are prepared to sacrifice their own interests for joint good.

THERE is another encouraging indication of cooperation in such projects as the Mekong River development plan, which is under United Nations auspices. Estimated to take 20 years to finish, the program aims to construct dams and hydroelectric plants, to expand fisheries and to improve navigation. Another hopeful scheme, initiated in 1965, was the Asian Development Bank, which began with a capital of $1 billion contributed largely by the United States and Japan.

But before the states of the area can begin to think seriously of regional pacts or such advanced ideas as, say, a common market, they must begin to deal more efficiently with their individual economic and political problems.

In recent years, much discussion has centered around the relative qualities of military versus civilian administration in underdeveloped countries. In Southeast Asia, the manner in which disciplined army officers can halt a trend toward political and economic disintegration is no better illustrated than by events in Burma from 1958 to 1960. The civilian government under Prime Minister U Nu, beset by bitter internal rivalries, appeared to be heading into civil war when General Ne Win peacefully assumed direction of the country. During two years in power, his cabinet of young colonels was successful in activities as divergent as reducing crime and ridding Rangoon of thousands of mangy dogs. Ne Win returned Burma to civilian rule following what he called his "caretaker" regime, but in 1962, when the politicians appeared to be moving toward disaster, he again took control.

Although they may appear attractive in emergencies, military governments do not provide a long-term solution to the problem of political stability in Southeast Asian states. A primary task of these young countries is to find forms of government suitable to their local necessities and characteristics. A political system suitable for a Southeast Asian state may not turn out to be a facsimile of a western democracy. But if it is genuine, legitimate and popular, the system is likely to be effective. The brilliant young Philippine Senator Raul Manglapus has eloquently outlined the need for a new set of political values reflecting the "genius of the people" and representing an authentic consensus.

In any real search for fresh political concepts, Southeast Asia's leaders should encourage the talents of younger men with new ideas. Too often, however, the old-guard nationalists who are in power resent the efforts of hopeful youths to participate in government activities. Consequently, political change in the region has often come brutally, in uprisings engineered by younger officials or military men who feel they cannot rise normally through the existing institutions. Their desire for personal advancement has, in large measure, stimulated violent change in South Vietnam and Indonesia, leaving the governments in those countries unstable.

ONLY with efficient, popular governments can the young countries of Southeast Asia begin to approach their complex economic and social tasks. Only through such governments can foreign aid, no matter how generous, have any effectiveness. Thus far, however, most of Southeast Asia's states show few signs of shaping solid, durable political institutions.

It appears probable that Southeast Asia will face continued turmoil and turbulence in the coming years. Whether the region can ultimately resist the multiple menaces of economic retrogression, political instability and communism is a question that even the most oracular astrologer would hesitate to answer. A Vietnamese official not long ago summed up an attitude about the future that many thoughtful Southeast Asians seem to share. "Perhaps it is pointless to be pessimistic," he said, "but it is difficult to be optimistic."

Heavy traffic swirls through downtown Djakarta. Next page: Village school children in Bali perch on the roots of a giant tree.

THRUST into the modern world, Southeast Asians are seeking new ways . . .

. . . to synthesize their ancient, leisurely paced and elaborately ceremonial cultures

with the complicated economic and political experience of the western nations

Appendix

HISTORICAL DATES

B.C.

- **3rd Century** — Buddhist missionaries are sent into Southeast Asia from India
- **c.200** — Kingdom of Nam-Viet founded in present-day northern Vietnam

A.D.

- **1st-2nd Centuries** — Rival kingdoms, both influenced by Hindu culture, develop in Funan (modern Cambodia) and Champa (central Vietnam)
- **6th or 7th Century** — Burmans from the Tibet-China border area migrate to modern Burma and gradually conquer earlier settlers. Later, they found the city of Pagan
- **7th Century** — Funan disintegrates. The Kingdom of Srivijaya evolves in south Sumatra and expands into Malaya
- **9th Century** — Sailendra Dynasty of Java gains control of Srivijaya kingdom
- **802** — Jayavarman II founds Angkor empire in Cambodia
- **1044-1287** — Pagan kingdom of Upper Burma annexes territories of Mon people in Lower Burma
- **1181-c.1220** — Jayavarman VII defeats Champa, expands the Angkor empire to include central Indochina
- **13th Century** — Mongol armies of Kublai Khan invade Southeast Asia. Moslem merchants from India build up a thriving trade between the Middle East and the Orient
- **1350** — Thai people moving south from China form a kingdom in present-day Thailand. A branch of the same stock founds the Lao kingdom of Lan Xang (Land of a Million Elephants) in 1353
- **1498** — Vasco da Gama and his Portuguese ships, having rounded the Cape of Good Hope, open new trade route and era of European expansion in Asia
- **1511** — Portuguese capture Malacca, Malayan seaport from which they later gain other Asian footholds
- **1521** — Ferdinand Magellan discovers and claims the Philippines for Spain during his expedition's world-circling voyage
- **16th Century** — Britain, France and the Netherlands join in the European race to dominate Asian trade. Government-chartered companies are formed. Each of them develops commercial spheres of influence in the area
- **1757** — Final unification of Burma
- **1777-1802** — Aided by French volunteers, Emperor Gia-Long unites Vietnam
- **1782** — Founder of present Chakri Dynasty of Thailand establishes a new capital at Bangkok
- **1811-1816** — The British occupy Java and other Dutch possessions during Napoleonic wars. Stamford Raffles, as the British lieutenant governor of Java, attempts administrative reforms. Territories revert to the Netherlands in the European peace settlement
- **1819** — Raffles founds the British colony of Singapore
- **1824** — Dutch cede all rights in Malaya to the British in return for cession of British rights in Indonesia
- **1824-1826** — British invade Burma to quell disturbances along Indian border
- **1862-1867** — Cochin China (southern Vietnam) becomes a French colony
- **1864** — French establish protectorate over Cambodia
- **1867** — Thailand receives disputed territories from Cambodia in return for its recognition of French suzerainty over Cambodia
- **1883-1885** — French protectorate established over Annam and Tonkin
- **1887-1893** — Colony of Cochin China and protectorates of Annam, Tonkin, Cambodia and Laos organized as French Indochina under a governor-general
- **1895** — Federated Malay States formed, and a British resident-general is appointed
- **1898-1899** — Spanish-American War. In the peace treaty Spain cedes the Philippines to the U.S., but Filipinos, having declared independence from Spain and elected a president, commence fighting with U.S. occupation forces. They continue guerrilla warfare until 1902
- **1911-1912** — Moslem merchants in Java found Sarekat Islam (Islamic Association) which develops into a nationalist movement protesting Dutch rule
- **1927** — Sukarno emerges as nationalist leader in Indonesia
- **1939-1945** — World War II. Japanese take over Southeast Asia, utilizing slogan "Asia for the Asians" and ruling through occupation or puppet governments. Japan's defeat in 1945 leaves area in ferment over independence
- **1945** — Nationalists proclaim the independence of Indonesia, but the Dutch refuse to grant it. Forces of the Viet Minh, Vietnamese nationalist group formed in China during the war and led by Ho Chi Minh, occupy Hanoi and declare Vietnam independent
- **1946** — Philippines granted independence
- **1946-1954** — Hostility between France and the Viet Minh erupts into full-scale war. After the French military bastion at Dien Bien Phu falls, Vietnam is divided along the 17th parallel. French-installed Emperor Bao Dai heads South Vietnam's government. North Vietnam is organized as a Communist state
- **1948** — Burma wins independence, rejects membership in the British Commonwealth. Communist guerrilla action threatens Malaya's government
- **1949** — Following United Nations intervention, the Dutch transfer full sovereignty to the republican government of Indonesia. Cambodia and Laos are recognized as independent states associated with France
- **1953-present** — The pro-communist Pathet Lao movement organizes a "free government" in northern Laos in opposition to the royal government. Brief periods of cooperation alternate with outbursts of fighting
- **1955** — After the ouster of Emperor Bao Dai, Ngo Dinh Diem becomes South Vietnam's president
- **1957** — Federation of Malaya joins British Commonwealth as an independent state
- **1963** — South Vietnam's Ngo Dinh Diem is killed in army coup; internal disturbances and communist guerrilla activity cause increase in U.S. armed assistance. The state of Malaysia comes into being, consisting of the Federation of Malaya, and the British dependencies of Singapore, North Borneo and Sarawak
- **1965** — Singapore secedes from Malaysia to become independent
- **1967** — President Sukarno of Indonesia loses all governmental powers; General Suharto becomes president. Number of U.S. servicemen fighting in Vietnam rises above 450,000

FOR FURTHER READING

CHAPTER 1: A MOSAIC OF PEOPLES

Blanchard, Wendell, ed., *Thailand.* HRAF Press, 1958.

Buss, Claude, *Southeast Asia and the World Today.* D. Van Nostrand, 1958.

Cressey, George B., *Asia's Lands and Peoples.* McGraw-Hill, 1951.

Dobby, E.H.G., *Monsoon Asia.* Quadrangle Books, 1961.

Du Bois, Cora, *Social Forces in Southeast Asia.* Harvard University Press, 1959.

East, W. G., and O.H.K. Spate, eds., *The Changing Map of Asia.* E. P. Dutton, 1959.

Forster, Harold, *Flowering Lotus; A View of Java.* Longmans, Green, 1958.

Ginsburg, Norton, ed., *The Pattern of Asia.* Prentice-Hall, 1958.

Hall, D.G.E., *Burma.* Hutchinson's University Library, London, 1950.

Le Bar, Frank M., and Adrienne Suddard, eds., *Laos.* HRAF Press, 1960.

Lewis, Norman, *A Dragon Apparent; Travels in Indo-China.* Charles Scribner's Sons, 1951. *Golden Earth: Travels in Burma.* Charles Scribner's Sons, 1952.

Meeker, Oden, *The Little World of Laos.* Charles Scribner's Sons, 1959.

Michael, Franz H., and George E. Taylor, *The Far East in the Modern World.* Henry Holt, 1956.

Murdock, George Peter, ed., *Social Structure in Southeast Asia.* Quadrangle Books, 1960.

Robequain, Charles, *Malaya, Indonesia, Borneo and the Philippines.* Longmans, Green, 1958.

Spencer, J. E., *Asia, East by South.* John Wiley & Sons, 1954.

CHAPTER 2: EARLY HISTORY AND MIGRATIONS

Cole, Fay Cooper, *The People of Malaysia.* D. Van Nostrand, 1945.

Collis, Maurice, *The Land of the Great Image.* New Directions, 1959.

Fitzgerald, Charles P., *China, A Short Cultural History.* Frederick A. Praeger, 1954.

Hall, D.G.E., *A History of South-East Asia.* St. Martin's Press, 1961.

Harrison, Brian, *South-East Asia, A Short History.* St. Martin's Press, 1960.

Weins, Herold J., *China's March Toward the Tropics.* Shoe String Press, 1954.

Winstedt, Richard, *The Malays: A Cultural History.* Routledge & Kegan Paul, London, 1947.

Young, Gordon, *The Hill Tribes of Northern Thailand.* Siam Society, Bangkok, 1962.

CHAPTER 3: THE COLONIAL ERA

Buttinger, Joseph, *The Smaller Dragon.* Frederick A. Praeger, 1958.

Collis, Maurice, *Siamese White.* Faber & Faber, London, 1936.

Edwardes, Michael, *Asia in the European Age, 1498-1955.* Thames and Hudson, London, 1961.

Furnivall, J. S., *Colonial Policy and Practice.* New York University Press, 1956.

Harvey, G. E., *British Rule in Burma.* Faber & Faber, London, 1956.

Herz, Martin F., *A Short History of Cambodia.* Frederick A. Praeger, 1958.

Hobson, John A., *Imperialism.* Macmillan, 1933.

Jacoby, Eric H., *Agrarian Unrest in Southeast Asia.* Asia Publishing House, Bombay, 1961.

Kennedy, J., *A History of Malaya.* St. Martin's Press, 1962.

Moffat, Abbot L., *Mongkut: The King of Siam.* Cornell University Press, 1961.

Orwell, George, *Burmese Days.* Harcourt, Brace and World, 1950.

Panikkar, Kavalam M., *Asia and Western Dominance.* Hillary House Publishers, 1959.

Priestley, Herbert Ingram, *France Overseas Through the Old Régime.* University of California Press, 1939.

Runciman, Steven, *The White Rajahs: A History of Sarawak from 1841 to 1946.* Cambridge University Press, 1960.

Vlekke, Bernard H. M., *Nusantara: A History of Indonesia.* Quadrangle Books, 1959.

Zaide, Gregorio F., *Philippine Political and Cultural History.* Two vols. Philippine Education, Manila, 1949.

CHAPTER 4: NATIONALIST MOVEMENTS

Crozier, Brian, *The Rebels.* Beacon Press, 1960.

Elsbree, Willard H., *Japan's Role in Southeast Asian Nationalist Movememts.* Harvard University Press, 1953.

Emerson, Rupert, *From Empire to Nation.* Harvard University Press, 1960.

Fifield, Russell H., *The Diplomacy of Southeast Asia: 1945-58.* Harper & Brothers, 1958.

Fischer, Louis, *The Story of Indonesia: Old Land, New Nation.* Harper & Brothers, 1959.

Hammer, Ellen, *The Struggle for Indochina.* Stanford University Press, 1954.

Jones, Francis C., *Japan's New Order in East Asia.* Oxford University Press, 1954.

Lancaster, Donald, *The Emancipation of French Indochina.* Oxford University Press, 1961.

Miller, Harry, *Prince and Premier; A Biography of Tunku Abdul Rahman.* George G. Harrap, London, 1959.

Palma, Rafael, *The Pride of the Malay Race; A Biography of José Rizal.* Prentice-Hall, 1949.

Tinker, Hugh, *The Union of Burma.* Oxford University Press, 1959.

Wehl, David, *The Birth of Indonesia.* George Allen & Unwin, London, 1949.

Wolff, Leon, *Little Brown Brother.* Doubleday, 1961.

Woodman, Dorothy, *The Making of Burma.* Cresset Press, London, 1962. *The Republic of Indonesia.* Cresset Press, London, 1955.

CHAPTER 5: EXPECTATIONS AND ILLUSIONS

Almond, Gabriel A., and James S. Coleman, eds., *The Politics of the Developing Areas.* Princeton University Press, 1960.

Busch, Noel F., *Thailand.* D. Van Nostrand, 1959.

Butwell, Richard, *Southeast Asia Today—and Tomorrow.* Frederick A. Praeger, 1961.

Cady, John F., *A History of Modern Burma.* Cornell University Press, 1958.

De Young, John E., *Village Life in Modern Thailand.* University of California Press, 1958.

Emerson, Rupert, *Representative Government in Southeast Asia.* Harvard University Press, 1955.

Golay, Frank, *Public Policy and National Economic Development: The Philippines.* Cornell University Press, 1961.

Hanna, Willard A., *Bung Karno's Indonesia.* American Universities Field Staff, 1960.

Kahin, George, ed., *Governments and Politics of Southeast Asia.* Cornell University Press, 1959. *Nationalism and Revolution in Indonesia.* Cornell University Press, 1952.

Kaufman, Howard Keva, *Bangkhuad; A Community Study in Thailand.* J. J. Augustin, 1960.

Khaing, Mi Mi, *Burmese Family.* Indiana University Press, 1962.

Mills, Lennox A., *Malaya: A Political and Economic Appraisal.* University of Minnesota Press, 1958.

Sjahrir, Soetan, *Out of Exile.* John Day, 1949.

Vandenbosch, Amry, and Richard Butwell, *The Changing Face of Southeast Asia.* University of Kentucky Press, 1966.

Wertheim, William F., *Indonesian Society in Transition.* W. Van Hoeve, The Hague, 1956.

Wilson, David A., *Politics in Thailand.* Cornell University Press, 1962.

CHAPTER 6: THE ARTS

Bowers, Faubion, *Theatre in the East.* Grove Press, 1960.

Briggs, Lawrence Palmer, *The Ancient Khmer Empire.* American Philosophical Society, 1951.

Covarrubias, Miguel, *Island of Bali.* Alfred A. Knopf, 1937.

Groslier, Bernard, *The Arts and Civilization of Angkor.* Frederick A. Praeger, 1957.

Le May, Reginald, *The Culture of South-East Asia.* George Allen & Unwin, London, 1954.

Modern Art of Asia. Toto Shuppan, Tokyo, 1961.

The Arts of Thailand. Indiana University, 1960.

Wagner, Frits A., *Art of the World, Indonesia.* McGraw-Hill, 1959.

Zimmer, Heinrich, *Myths and Symbols in Indian Art and Civilization.* Harper & Brothers, 1962.

CHAPTER 7: RELIGION

Burtt, Edwin A., *The Teachings of the Compassionate Buddha*. New American Library of World Literature, 1955.

Conze, Edward, *Buddhist Scriptures*. Penguin Books, 1959.

Durant, Will, *The Story of Civilization; Our Oriental Heritage*. Simon and Schuster, 1954.

Eliot, Charles, *Hinduism and Buddhism: An Historical Sketch*. Three vols. Barnes & Noble, 1954.

Geertz, Clifford, *The Religion of Java*. Free Press, 1959.

Gibb, H.A.R., *Mohammedanism: An Historical Survey*. Oxford University Press, 1953.

Humphreys, Christmas, *Buddhism*. Penguin Books, 1958.

Landon, Kenneth P., *Southeast Asia: Crossroad of Religions*. University of Chicago Press, 1949.

Morgan, Kenneth W., *The Path of the Buddha*. Ronald Press, 1956.

Rajadhon, Phya Anuman, *Life and Ritual in Old Siam*. HRAF Press, 1961.

Thomas, Edward J., *The History of Buddhist Thought*. Barnes & Noble, 1951.

Von Grunebaum, Gustave E., ed., *Unity and Variety in Muslim Civilization*. University of Chicago Press, 1955.

CHAPTER 8: THE OVERSEAS CHINESE

Coughlin, Richard J., *Double Identity: The Chinese in Modern Thailand*. Oxford University Press, 1960.

Elegant, Robert, *The Dragon's Seed*. St. Martin's Press, 1959.

Mitchison, Lois, *The Overseas Chinese*. The Bodley Head, London, 1961.

Purcell, Victor, *The Chinese in Southeast Asia*, 2nd ed. Oxford University Press, 1965.

Skinner, G. William, *Leadership and Power in the Chinese Community of Thailand*. Cornell University Press, 1958.

Thompson, Virginia and Richard Adloff, *Minority Problems in Southeast Asia*. Stanford University Press, 1955.

Williams, Lea E., *The Future of the Overseas Chinese in Southeast Asia*. McGraw-Hill, 1966.

CHAPTER 9: COMMUNISM

Brimmell, J. H., *Communism in South East Asia*. Oxford University Press, 1959.

Champassak, Sisouk Na, *Storm over Laos*. Frederick A. Praeger, 1961.

Fall, Bernard B., *Street Without Joy*. rev. ed. Stackpole, 1966.

Kennedy, Malcolm D., *History of Communism in Asia*. Frederick A. Praeger, 1956.

Thompson, Robert, *Defeating Communist Insurgency*. Chatto & Windus, London, 1966.

Trager, Frank N., ed., *Marxism in Southeast Asia*. Stanford University Press, 1959.

Warner, Denis, *Hurricane from China*. Macmillan, 1961.

CHAPTER 10: THE FUTURE

Gordon, Bernard K., *Dimensions of Conflict in Southeast Asia*. Prentice Hall, 1966.

POLITICAL UNITS IN SOUTHEAST ASIA (as of October 1, 1967)

NAME	POPULATION	AREA (in sq. mi.)	CAPITAL	GOVERNMENT
Brunei	104,000	2,226	Brunei	British-protected sultanate
Burma	25,246,000	261,689	Rangoon	Republic. Received independence from Great Britain in 1948
Cambodia	6,250,000	67,550	Phnom Penh	Monarchy. Granted independence by France in 1953
Indonesia	104,500,000	575,893	Djakarta	Republic. Independence granted by the Netherlands in 1949
Laos	635,000	91,482	Vientiane	Monarchy. Received independence from France in 1949
Malaysia	9,711,000	127,672	Kuala Lumpur	Federation, formed in 1963, including 11 states of Federation of Malaya and former British colonies of Sarawak and North Borneo (now Sabah). Member of the British Commonwealth
North Vietnam	19,000,000	61,516	Hanoi	Democratic Republic (under Communist control). Divided from South Vietnam in 1954
Singapore	1,914,000	225	Singapore	Republic. Separated from Malaysia in 1965. Member of the British Commonwealth
South Vietnam	16,124,000	65,709	Saigon	Republic. Divided from North Vietnam in 1954
Thailand	31,508,000	198,404	Bangkok	Monarchy
The Philippines	33,477,000	115,600	Quezon City	Republic. Given independence by the U.S. in 1946

GREAT ACHIEVEMENTS IN SOUTHEAST ASIAN CULTURE

COUNTRY	LOCATION	WORKS
Burma	Pagan	Ananda (1090), temple with a solid central block crowned by a four-sided tower. Four gilded Buddhas stand in a court enclosed by two galleries
		Kyaukku, cave-temple built into a steep ravine, with a great stone vault. Facing the entrance hall is a colossal seated Buddha. Lower story may date from Fifth Century; upper ones added in 12th Century
		Mahabodhi (c.1200), temple covered with niches holding images of the Buddha, interspersed with panels and moldings
		Shwezigon (begun 1059), cylindrical structure erected to contain sacred relics of the Buddha. Also enshrines the 37 principal *nats,* or spirits, of Burma
		Thatbyinnyu (1144), five stories high. Dominates all other temples at Pagan in majesty of line
	Pegu	Shwemawdaw, shrine traditionally dating from the Buddha's lifetime. Rebuilt after its destruction by earthquake in 1930
		Shwethalyaung (10th Century), gilded reclining Buddha, lost for many years in the jungle, is 180 feet long and 46 feet high at the shoulder
	Rangoon	Shwe Dagon, one of the greatest Buddhist shrines in Asia, whose date of construction is lost in legend. The circular base is surrounded by smaller pagodas and temples and crowned by a great gold spire
Cambodia	Banam	Prasat Preah Toc (Funan period, c.1-550 A.D.), brick structures without ornamentation
	Sambor	Sambor-Prei Kuk (Chenla period, c.550-800), brick structures with low relief sculpture
	Angkor	Angkor Thom (12th-13th Centuries), the walled capital city entered through four-faced gate towers supported by three-headed elephants. Gods and demons, holding a serpent, guard the Gate of Victory. Bayon temple is in the center of the city
		Angkor Wat (c.1113-1150), the greatest and best-preserved of Khmer monuments, renowned for its size and decorations. Notable details are the expanse of bas-relief along the outer gallery and serpent heads carved from a single block of stone
		Banteai Srei (10th Century), Citadel of Women, a small red sandstone-faced temple with carved *frontons* depicting Hindu legends
Indonesia	Bali	Besaki (14th Century), mountain sanctuary of the Gélgél kingdom. An 11-story "mountain of heaven"
		Panataran Sasih at Pédjéng, harboring the Bronze Age "Moon of Bali" kettledrum
	Java	Borobudur (c.800), the most impressive monument remaining from the Sailendra kingdom. A natural mound of earth is enclosed by a massive series of stone terraces surmounted by a spire. Reliefs along the lower terrace walls illustrate the life of the Buddha
		Chandi Khalasan (778), Sailendra temple dedicated to the Buddhist goddess, Tara
		Chandi Mendut (c.850), another Sailendra monument whose interior sculptures have been well-preserved, including a stone seated Buddha
		Prambanan, a group of shrines surrounding Loro Jonggrang (c.915), the principal temple. It is dedicated to Shiva; lesser ones honor Vishnu and Brahma. Bas-relief sculpture is outstanding in Javanese art
Laos	Luang Prabang	Wat Visoun (1503), monastery housing sculpture and images from the 12th Century
	Vientiane	That Luang (16th Century), historic shrine for purported relics of the Buddha
Thailand	Bangkok	Wat Phra Keo (1785), temple in the compound of the Grand Palace, built to house the sacred Emerald Buddha
		Wat Benchamabopit (1899), rebuilt on the site of an older temple by King Chulalongkorn. Utilizes Italian marble and Chinese glazed tile. Contains a large collection of images of the Buddha from all the countries of the Far East
		Wat Po (1789), chapel housing an enormous reclining Buddha with inlaid mother-of-pearl in the soles of the feet
	Lampun	Wat Kukuta (rebuilt in 1218), a slender pyramid of five stories, one of the few remaining monuments of Dvaravati architecture
	Sukhodaya	Maha-Tat (13th Century?) depicting Buddhist scenes in stucco relief
		Wat Si Chum (14th Century?) with stone slab engravings of Jataka legends
Vietnam	Hué	Tu Doc (1867), one of many ornate royal tombs
	Nha Trang	Po Nagar (Seventh Century), quadrangular brick towers, remnants of a Cham sanctuary, with elaborately carved altars and stone decorations

Credits

The sources for the illustrations in this book are shown below: Credits for pictures from left to right are separated by commas, top to bottom by dashes.

Cover: Ernst Haas from Magnum
8, 9—Henri Cartier-Bresson from Magnum
10—Map by Enrico Arno
16—Henri Cartier-Bresson from Magnum
17—Ernst Haas from Magnum
18, 19—Maynard Frank Wolfe
20, 21—Ernst Haas from Magnum
22, 23—René Burri from Magnum, Marc & Evelyne Bernheim from Rapho Guillumette—Ted Spiegel from Rapho Guillumette
24—John Dominis
25, 26, 27—Henri Cartier-Bresson from Magnum
29—Map by Bill Dove
33—Ernst Haas from Magnum
34, 35—Eliot Elisofon
36—John Lewis Stage from Lensgroup
37—Howard Sochurek
38, 39—John Dominis
40, 41—From Theodor Debry's *Small Voyages* Part 8, published in Frankfurt 1607, courtesy The Rare Book Division, New York Public Library
44—Map by Enrico Arno
49—Jack Birns
50, 51—Howard Sochurek, James Burke
52—Dolf Herras
53—Marc Riboud from Magnum
54, 55—John Dominis, Jerry Cooke
56—Howard Sochurek
65—John Launois from Black Star
66, 67—Lisa Larsen, Charles Bonay, Le Minh, Associated Press Photo from New York, James Pickerell from Black Star
68, 69—Right Lewis Kraar—United Press International
70—Jacob Loke, Michel Renard—Harry Redl from Black Star, Francis Miller
71—Co Rentmeester—Burke Uzzle from Magnum
72—John Dominis
79—John Bulmer, Camera Press-Pix London
80—Henri Cartier-Bresson from Magnum—Howard Sochurek
81—Edward W. Lollis
82, 83—Ted Polumbaum
84—Henri Cartier-Bresson from Magnum
85, 86, 87—John Dominis
88, 89—Henri Cartier-Bresson from Magnum
92, 93—Drawings by Nel Van Dam from Frits A. Wagner's *Indonesia* in the series Kunst Der Welt, Holle Verlag Baden-Baden, Germany
96 through 100—Henri Cartier-Bresson from Magnum
101, 102, 103—Walter Sanders courtesy Department of Fine Arts, Bangkok
104—Howard Sochurek
107—Drawing by Enrico Arno
111—Jack Birns
112—Henri Cartier-Bresson from Magnum
113—Marc Riboud from Magnum
114—John Dominis
115—Ernst Haas from Magnum
116—John Dominis, Howard Sochurek
117—Howard Sochurek
118, 119—John Dominis
120—Ewing Krainin
127 through 129—Howard Sochurek
130—Howard Sochurek—Larry Burrows
131—Howard Sochurek
132, 133—John Launois from Black Star
139—Wide World Photos
140—Wide World Photos—Lee Lockwood from Black Star
141—Lee Lockwood from Black Star
142, 143—Wide World Photos, Horst Faas for Wide World—Burke Uzzle from Magnum
144, 145—Henri Cartier-Bresson from Magnum
149—Co Rentmeester
150, 151—Henri Cartier-Bresson from Magnum

ACKNOWLEDGMENTS

The editors of this book are indebted to Lionel Landry, Associate Director of The Asia Society, and to Dr. Lauriston Sharp, Professor of Anthropology and Asian Studies, Cornell University. Both read and commented in detail on portions of the text.

Index

** This symbol in front of a page number indicates a photograph or painting of the subject mentioned.*

Diem, Ngo Dinh, 51, 62 *66; regime of, in Vietnam, 14, 64